A Little Touch
of Heaven

FOR WOMEN

New Leaf Press

A Little Touch of Heaven

FOR WOMEN

by

ROBERT STRAND

First printing: February 1997

Copyright © 1997 by New Leaf Press. All rights reserved. Printed in the United States of America. No part of this book may be used or reproduced in any manner whatsoever without written permission of the publisher except in the case of brief quotations in articles and reviews. For information write: New Leaf Press, Inc., P.O. Box 726, Green Forest, AR 72638.

ISBN: 0-89221-345-0
Library of Congress Number: 97-65167

Dedication

To my wife, Donna, who has taught me all I have learned about women.

1.
THE CREATION OF MOTHERS

When the Lord was creating the very first "mother," He was already into overtime when the angel made an appearance. The angel took in the scene and said, "You're doing quite a lot of fiddling around on this model."

And the Lord replied, "Have you been reading the specs on this one? She has to be completely washable . . . but not plastic. Must have 180 different moving parts . . . which can be replaced or backed up. She must run on black coffee and kids' leftovers. She must have a lap that disappears when she stands up. She must be able to convey love with a look. She must be flexible . . . but resilient and strong. She must be able to run at top speed even if she has been up the entire past night with a sick child. And . . . have a kiss which can cure everything from a broken arm to a disappointed love affair. Oh yes, and six pairs of hands."

The angel shook her head slowly and said, "Six pairs of hands . . . there is no way."

"Well, it's not really the hands that are causing the problems," said the Lord. "It's the extra pairs of eyes that every mother must be equipped with."

"All of that has to be on the standard model?" asked the angel.

The Lord nodded, then continued, "One pair of eyes that can see through closed doors so that when she asks, 'What are you kids doing in there?' she already knows. Then there must be another set of eyes in the back of her head that can see what she is not supposed to see, but what she has to see to know what is going on back there. Then, of course, there are the ones here in the front, the standard issue, so that she can look at a child who has messed up and say with those eyes, 'I understand and I love you' without so much as uttering another word."

"Lord," said the angel, reaching gently for His sleeve, "come away for a while, get another perspective . . . get back to it tomorrow."

"Not yet, I just can't," said the Lord, "I'm so close to creating something so very close to myself.

Already I have one who heals herself when she is sick . . . knows how to feed a family of six on a single pound of hamburger . . . can drive a car and correct a child and make out a grocery list at the same time . . . who can completely gain her senses before her feet touch the floor in the middle of a night in answer to a child's cry . . . and can get a ten-year-old boy to stand under a shower with a bar of soap."

The angel circled the finished model of the first mother very slowly. "It's too soft," the angel pointed out.

"But tough! Resilient! Patient! Perseverant!" said the Lord, excitedly. "You cannot possibly imagine what this mother and all the other mothers which will follow her can do or endure."

"Can this mother think?"

"Not only think . . . but she can reason, compromise, negotiate, cajole, persuade, and use logic."

Finally, the angel bent over and ran her finger over the cheek. "There's a leak," she pronounced. "I think You are attempting to put too much into this first model."

"That's not a leak," replied the Lord. "It's something new, it's a tear."

"Well, what is a tear for?"

"Tears are to express joy and sadness, disappointment and achievement, pain and triumph, loneliness and ecstasy, happiness and hurt, pride and discouragement. . . ."

"Lord, You've done it again, You are a genius," said the angel.

The Lord looked somber, "I didn't put the tear there."[1]

There's an old proverb from Spain that goes something like this, "God couldn't be everywhere so He created mothers."

How true! What a high, holy, and exciting calling . . . to be a mother! And when does a woman become a mother? Does it happen at birth? Does it happen in childhood or adolescent or adulthood? Is it innate? Or does it happen when the woman carries a live and growing person inside her body? Does it happen at the moments of birth, of pain and struggle to bring forth a new life into this world? Or is it a process which begins with the birth of a girl-child and is nurtured by her own mother and aunts who are mothers and grandmothers who are mothers?

Whenever it happens we may not be exactly sure . . . but that it happens is a cause for joy and happiness. What would this world be like without mothers? None of us would be here without mothers! It's the opportunity to enter into partnership with God in the procreation of a new life. It goes beyond simply giving birth or being a biological mother . . . it's a lifetime calling to nurture and care and love each child into adulthood where it starts all over again when the mother becomes a grandmother.

Motherhood is not meant to be a solo flight, however. There is to be a life-partner who also is part of the process. And most importantly there is a Heavenly Father who stands ready to help when and where the call to help comes from a mother.

So . . . Mom, hold your head high, put your shoulders back, and live your life and fulfill your role with justifiable pride . . . and give God praise for the way in which you have been trusted to mold and prepare another life for here as well as for eternity.

TODAY'S BIBLE READING: Genesis 1:1-31

2
THE TOUCH THAT MAKES A DIFFERENCE

The human touch is incredibly therapeutic! Touching and being touched are important parts of life and living. In fact, studies have shown that if an infant doesn't experience touching very early in life, that life is endangered, even threatened by death. We need personal contact.

Years ago, in hospital nurseries, newborns were not to be touched except in emergencies. Dr. John Holt noted an incredible proportion of infant deaths. He believed there was a link between the failure to touch and the high death rates. He felt that the will to live is directly related to the experience of being held and touched as an infant. Dr. Holt instructed his neo-natal nurses to give "tender loving care" to six infants five times a day . . . to hold them, cuddle them, physically conveying love through touching. There was an immediate turn-around in infant deaths.

Today it's standard procedure, within moments after birth infants are placed in the mother's or father's arms. It makes a difference!

A simple, tiny woman named Mother Teresa has been awarded a Nobel Prize for her work in Calcutta among members of India's lowest caste. She seeks the least redeemable, the dying, from the gutters and garbage dumps of Calcutta's alleys and brings them to her hospital and surrounds them with touching love. The beggars, often too weak to talk, stare wide-eyed at the love that has come into their wretched lives. Have they died and gone to heaven, they wonder.

When she has been asked "Why?" Mother Teresa answers softly, "These people have been treated like dogs. Their greatest disease is a sense that they are unwanted. Don't they have the right to die like angels?"

Children who grow up in homes where there is very little touching are often withdrawn in character and personality in adulthood, retreating into a world of fantasy and too often express hostility to others and to the world at large. But when kids come from homes with lots of touching, hugging, kissing . . . they tend to grow up to be open and warm human beings. We need to be touched and touch others if our lives are to be all they ought to be.

And right here is a clue as to why God came to dwell among us. He understands this deep human need, because we have been created with it. We need a mother's touch . . . but we also need the touch of God. By God himself! We need to know His loving, caring touch, so God became flesh, taking upon himself human flesh and blood so He could live among humans. I believe God came in this form of flesh in order to touch us because touching is the highest form of communication. Words are fundamental to communication . . . but there are times when words fail us and a touch is the only way to communicate what the tongue cannot.

When Jesus came to live among us we were introduced to an entirely different picture of God. We saw a family . . . God the Father, God the Son, as they interacted. Jesus was born into a humble human family: a mother, Mary; a human father, Joseph; brothers and sisters. Do you realize that up until Jesus came on the scene we, the human race, had no idea that God was a caring, loving, Heavenly Father? Fathers tend to treat us differently than mere gods. Fathers hurt, sorrow, can be approached, care about socks and food and providing, as well as being vulnerable. Now that's the kind of a God that all of us can serve.

God is for life! God is for you! And this Almighty cares about you. You are important! You are special! You are rare . . . you are the only one of a kind!

Have you even given any thought to how special you really are? At the moment of conception, from all the possible combinations at God's command, He could have created 300 thousand billion different humans! This was from the possible choices of genes and chromosomes from your father and mother. Each of the other combinations would have ended with another complete human being. So when at the moment of the uniting of two cells which became you . . . there is not another in the whole world, never has been, never will be, exactly like you! You are a priceless treasure because of your rarity! The rarest of the rare! The only one in the world!

How does one go about becoming a mother? One way is by being able to see how to relate to a child, how to meet the needs of that child, how to set that child on the right course. Jesus did all of the above through a touch, and you'll remember how in the story of two blind men sitting by the roadside. They heard that Jesus was going by and they shouted, "Lord, Son of David, have mercy on us!" That got the attention of God in human form that day. He stopped and specifically asked them, "What do you want me to do for you?" What a question; just think about it. Does it apply to you, today? "Lord," they said, "we want our sight!" Now here's our line of specific interest, "Jesus had compassion on them and TOUCHED their eyes!"

How is it possible to really love and never touch? God dwelt among us and taught us that the ideal way to give love is through a touch and to receive love through a touch.

In 1956, Dr. Margaret Brand, an ophthalmologist and a member of a medical team, went into an area of India that had been devastated by drought for five years. The wells were drying up, crops had failed, hunger was everywhere. As soon as this primitive medical help camp had been set up, people straggled in from every direction, primarily begging for food. Many assumed they would have to stay in the camp to receive food. Many also volunteered for needless surgery on the belief that if they underwent surgery they would also receive food. Some even asked to have an eye removed in order to be given some food.

Many of the young Indian boys volunteered to assist at the camp. Dr. Margaret was assigned a shy, skinny, dark-skinned boy, about 12 years of age. He stood on a box, with an impressive but baggy hospital gown wrapped around him, and he was charged with strict instructions as to how to hold a three-cell flashlight so that the light beamed directly on the cornea of the patient's eyes for cataract surgery to take place. Margaret was a bit dubious . . . could a young Indian village boy, who had never watched any kind of a surgical procedure be able to endure the trauma of watching people's eyes sliced open and stitched together again?

This young boy performed his task with remarkable skill. During the first five operations he scrupulously followed Margaret's instructions on when to shift the angle of light, aiming the beam with a steady hand.

But during the sixth case he faltered, the beam wandered, the beam shook. Margaret kept reminding him, softly, "Little brother, show the light properly," which he would momentarily do, but soon it again would bob away from the operating field. Margaret could see that he simply could not bear to look at the eye being worked on. She finally stopped and asked if he was not feeling well.

Tears ran down his cheeks and he stuttered, "Oh, doctor . . . I . . . I . . . cannot look. This one, she is my mother."

Ten days later, the boy's suffering was really over. His mother's stitches were removed and the team gave her eyeglasses. She at first tried to blink away the dazzling light of day but finally adjusted, focused, and for the first time in her life saw her son. A broad smile creased her face as she reached out to touch him. "My son," she said, "I thought I knew you, but today I see you." And she pulled him close and held him.[2]

The Master's touch provided sight to two needy blind men. What could His touch do for you, today? But perhaps more importantly, mother, what could your touch do for someone else, today?

TODAY'S BIBLE READING: Matthew 20:20-34

3.
I HAD THE WORLD'S MEANEST MOTHER

"I had the meanest mother in all the world," writes a housewife who is now raising a family of her own. She continues, "While other kids ate candy and donuts for breakfast, I had to have hot cereal, eggs and bacon, or toast. When others had Cokes and Twinkies for lunch, I had to eat a nutritious sandwich with a piece of fruit. As you can guess, my supper was different than the other kids as well, we had to sit down together and stay seated until we were all finished . . . along with the insult of having to eat a square meal complete with veggies. We were not allowed to talk with a mouth full of food nor were we to interrupt anybody else who may have been talking. But at least I wasn't alone in all my early sufferings. My sister and my two brothers had the same mean mother as I did.

"My mother insisted upon knowing where we were at all times. You'd have thought that we were members of a chain gang or something like that. She had to know who our friends were and who their parents were and what we were doing. She insisted that if we said we'd be gone an hour, that we be gone one hour or less . . . not one hour and two minutes!

"We had to wear clean clothes and take a bath or shower every day! The other kids were allowed to wear their clothes for days at a time. Then to add insult to injury, we were subjected to the very highest of insults because she made some of our clothes herself, just to save the family money. No wearing of 'designer' jeans or shirts because they cost too much.

"The worst is yet to come. We had to be in bed by nine every night and up by seven on school days and no later than eight on non-school days. We just couldn't sleep till noon like our other friends. So while they slept till noon, my mother actually had the nerve to break all kinds of child labor laws. She made us work.

We had to wash dishes, make beds, change sheets on beds, learn to cook, carry out the garbage, mow the lawn, run errands, learn how to iron clothes, and all sorts of cruel and inhumane things. I was positive that she lay awake at night just to think of mean things to make us do.

"By the time we were teenagers, she was somewhat wiser and our lifestyle became even more unbearable. None of this tooting the horn of a car for us to come running out to the car. She embarrassed us to no end by making our dates and our friends come to the door for us. If I spent the night with a girl friend . . . can you just imagine, she would check up on me to see if I were really there. How embarrassing. I never had the chance to elope to Mexico or another state . . . that is, if I'd had a boyfriend to elope with.

"But on through the years, things didn't improve one bit. We could not stay home from school and lie in bed 'sick,' like some of our friends did to miss school. If our friends had a toe-ache, a hang-nail, a simple cold, were too tired, or some other such serious ailments . . . they could stay at home and not go to school. Not us, we had to go anyway, hurting or not, healthy or not, complaining or not.

"My mother was a complete failure as a mother. Out of her four children, all of us went on to attain some higher education. Not a one of us four has ever been arrested, divorced, or beats up on his or her mate. Each of my brothers took a turn and served in a branch of the armed services of this country.

"Oh, yes, I almost forgot . . . when Sunday came around and our friends were still in bed till noon, we had to get all dressed up in ill-fitting Sunday clothes, study our Sunday school lessons, bring an offering, and sit in church without talking so we could listen and participate. We had to endure family devotions before each evening meal . . . it was so embarrassing when our friends ate with us, they were subjected to this form of torture, too. We were not allowed to shoot off our mouths, we were not allowed to sass back, we were not allowed to curse or swear. We had to say 'thank you' and 'please' all the time. We were forced to show respect to others, our leaders, and our country . . . but especially to older people. Can you imagine, she forced us to stand when an older person entered the room!

"And whom do we blame for the terrible way in which we turned out? You're right! Our mean mother. But you can also look at some of the things we missed out on doing. We never got to march in a protest parade. We never got to take part in a riot. We never got to smoke pot or experiment with drugs. We never had the privilege of smoking or drinking anything stronger than a Coke . . . as well as a million and one other things that all of our friends got to do. Not a one of us was ever allowed to stay out all night at a party, just think of it!

"Imagine . . . she forced and disciplined us to grow up into mature God-fearing, educated, caring, honest, loving, compassionate adults.

"Using my upbringing as a background, I am now trying to raise my own three children so that they can become productive citizens in this world. I stand a little taller and am filled with pride when my children call me a 'mean mother.' Because, as you can see, I thank and praise God, and my grandmother and grandfather — together they gave me the MEANEST MOTHER IN ALL THE WORLD!"[3]

TODAY'S BIBLE READING: Proverbs 1:8-33

4
THE DAUGHTERS
OF EVE

One mother writes: "One holiday, above all others, strikes fear in the hearts of mothers everywhere — Mother's Day! It's the day we stand up to be measured against the standards set forth on millions of greeting cards. On that day I usually wake up with a headache. Will anyone remember that I'm a mother? Did my behavior over the past year warrant a gift?"

Today is a fantastic day for mothers! Sadly to say, not always have we, the Church, our children, husbands, and fathers, given the ladies among us the support that we should have. But there are tremendous changes taking place in a woman's world and sphere of influence.

This is the day for godly women, godly mothers, to touch this world and be recognized as the vital participants they are, in and for the kingdom of God. This is the day and time for women everywhere to throw off the reproach of "Eve." Every woman knows, or so I've been told, that as soon as she can understand the meaning of "boy" or "girl," that somehow she shall be perceived as being the lesser in life, no matter her country or culture. She has been perceived as being the weaker, as being less capable, and not as intelligent as her counterpart. Why?

We go all the way back to the Garden of Eden for an answer. Following the sin of the pair on the ground, God said to Satan, "From now on you and the woman will be enemies" (Gen. 3:15;LB). Therefore, it only stands to reason that Satan will be doing all in his power to discredit his enemy, the woman. But remember that there is a caveat here. Always remember, Jesus said that "Satan is a liar and the father of all lies." Can he ever speak the truth? Everything he says is suspect, every philosophy he espouses is a lie. Do not believe the lie or the liar!

But from the beginning Eve, and consequently her daughters, have had the blame for the fall of the human race dumped on them. It started with the lie of Satan which was reinforced by Adam. The man said, "The WOMAN you put here with me . . . she gave me some fruit from the tree and I ate it" (Gen. 3:12).

Adam was the first to accuse, but not the last. Adam was not deceived because he made a conscious decision to partake with Eve of the forbidden fruit. And where was Adam when Eve was being tempted by the serpent? She had a very willing companion. Together they left the Garden of Eden, separated from God because of their sin. Women have suffered through the ages because of Eve's tragic mistake. Today it's time to throw off this reproach of Eve! Right? Right!!

We . . . both men and women have bought into this worldly system that lowers women in many ways. Women are a threat to this worldly system and dangerous to Satan's kingdom. They were fooled once but are now more prone to recognize the tactics used against them. They spot evil at work more quickly than do men. Women, with their greater sensitivity, also have a greater capacity for discernment and this causes satanic hatred to be shown toward them all the more.

Women have special characteristics that make them dangerous to this worldly system, but vitally important to the church of Jesus Christ. When Jesus came to this earth with His ministry, He gave us a whole new pattern for the treatment of women. In the original creation "God created man in his own image, in the image of God he created him; MALE AND FEMALE HE CREATED THEM. God blessed THEM and said to THEM . . ." (Gen. 1:27). Jesus came to restore what had been taken, what had been lost in the fall. "They all joined together constantly in prayer, along with the women and Mary the mother of Jesus, and with his brothers" (Acts 1:14). History was in the making, women were equal participants in this first church prayer meeting, as Eve had been an equal at the original creation. But it was tough for the men to acknowledge it. Read carefully this note: "In those days Peter stood up among the believers . . . and said, "Brothers, the Scripture had to be fulfilled." (Acts 1:15-16). He just couldn't bring himself to say, "Sisters and brothers."

But let's set this record straight once and for all. "There is neither Jew nor Greek, slave nor free, MALE NOR FEMALE, for YOU ARE ALL ONE IN CHRIST JESUS. If you belong to Christ, then you are Abraham's seed, and heirs according to the promise" (Gal. 3:28-29; caps are mine). When Jesus came, He set aside all the usual barriers which people are so prone to erect. He dashed all national distinctives, He set aside all class differences, and erased all gender divisions! We just read it! "YOU ARE ALL ONE IN CHRIST JESUS!" We are to be on level footing as we stand together about the cross of Calvary! He paid the price to set us all free of such distinctives! And the promise is that "whom the Son sets free is free indeed!"

TODAY'S BIBLE READING: Genesis 1:27–28

5.
THE OPPORTUNITY
TO BE A REAL SON

Leo Tolstoy often told old folk stories to challenge his listeners. One of his favorites is about an aged man who happened to overhear the conversations of three village peasant women drawing water at the communal well.

The first one to speak described her son in the most glowing terms . . . he was an entertainer! And what an entertainer, he surpassed all the others in his dexterity, skill, presentation, and ability to hold an audience.

The second of these three mothers, not be outdone, extolled her son's beautiful voice! With his wonderful tenor voice he could thrill the young and the old, he could create happy and sad moods in his listeners, the notes were sweet as the song of a nightingale.

Then the two turned to the third mother and asked, "In what kind of talent does your son excel?"

The woman simply replied, "My son is quite an ordinary boy who has no special gifts or talents of which I can report."

The old man then followed the three mothers on their way back to the village. Each bore two heavy buckets of water which made them stop for a rest. As they rested, their three sons came running to meet them. The first one turned one handspring followed by a somersault all the way down the path toward his mother. The women stood admiring the young entertainer.

The second son came toward his mother singing like that nightingale. His singing moved the mothers, each wiped away a tear because they were so moved.

The third son just ran to his mother, picked up the heavy buckets she had been carrying and he lugged them all the way home for her.

Then the three women inquired of the old man, "What do you have to say about our sons?" "Your sons?" responded the astonished man. "I saw only one son. I recognized only one real son."[4]

Mother . . . do you happen to remember the excitement of those months immediately before your first child was born? There are few scenes more delightful than to watch a young couple making their way through a department store looking at baby clothes and baby things. The young mother, obviously pregnant, holds up pink, ruffled clothes and shyly smiles at her young husband who is soon the father-to-be. It's one of those self-conscious moments. Then they move on to the boys section and he holds up jeans and sweatshirts. If they happen to be near the sporting goods he may pick up a baseball glove or a football or hockey stick. She watches him dream a bit.

And if you're careful, follow at a discreet distance as they saunter through the toy department and both . . . self-consciousness now gone . . . examine stuffed animals, baby car seats, strollers, disposable versus cloth diapers, and much more. This optimism and excitement that a newborn brings is one of the most encouraging parts of life!

Then the baby is born . . . more excitement, more first-time thrills, more plans as the child grows. Soon it's evident that in order for their child, your child, to become a mature, responsible human being it will take some doing, lots of wisdom, insight, guidance, and discipline in order to help that child become all that he or she can become. Turning that child into an adolescent who becomes an adult is a major process of discipline. So how do you turn a baby into a real son?

This message is too short to cover all the bases, but let's just look at one: DISCIPLINE! This is a huge subject fraught with lots of current concepts. There is one problem, you only get one chance with your child, you can't go back and do it all over again.

The obvious starting place is to be SELF-DISCIPLINED YOURSELF. How can you teach another to be disciplined if you're not disciplined yourself? Children will do as they are told only so long. They will follow an example much better than any set of spoken instructions.

Second, AGREE ON THE METHODS OF DISCIPLINE WITH YOUR SPOUSE. A house divided against itself cannot long stand. It will not take a child long to learn how to play one parent against the other, if you are not in agreement.

Third, START EARLY WITH DISCIPLINE. That wonderful, cuddly, bubbly, bundle of joy likely needs to learn that it can't have everything it wants when it wants it. The first thing mother Wesley taught her children was that they would get nothing by crying for it. With that lesson taught, she brought up 19 children and taught them all herself, besides attending to the details of raising a family of that size. Her discipline was the fountainhead from which the whole Methodist Church came! She gave John and Charles to the whole world and they made a difference. Win this battle early and life will be much more pleasant for you and your child.

Fourth, CONTINUOUS PERSEVERANCE WITH GOD'S HELP GETS THE JOB DONE. From the Old Testament we see this lesson plan given by God to the people of Israel. He was laying out foundational values upon which they were to build a new life in a new land of promise. "These are the commands, decrees, and laws the Lord your God directed me to teach you to observe in the land that you are crossing the Jordan to possess, SO THAT YOU, YOUR CHILDREN AND THEIR CHILDREN AFTER THEM MAY FEAR THE LORD YOUR GOD AS LONG AS YOU LIVE . . ." (Deut. 6:1-2). How to do that? "Impress them on your children. Talk about them when you sit at home and when you walk along the road, when you lie down and when you get up. Tie them as symbols on your hands and bind them on your foreheads. Write them on the doorframes of your houses and on your gates" (Deut. 6:7-9). Everything of life can be part of the ongoing discipline which results in children who will continue in living a disciplined life.

Motherhood is more than a birthing. It goes on until that child is mature enough to make his/her own way in the world, a disciplined child which brings delight, joy, and happiness to any parent!

Webster said: "If we work on marble, it will perish; if we work upon brass, time will efface it; but if we work upon immortal minds, if we imbue them with principles, with the just fear of God and love of our fellow men, we engrave on those tablets something which will brighten all eternity."

TODAY'S BIBLE READING:
  Deuteronomy 6:1–25

6.
IT'S TIME
FOR ACTION

Mothers come in all kinds of various sizes: skinny, tall, short, just right, and filled out. You can find them everywhere . . . start in maternity wards, changing diapers, washing clothes, working over ironing boards, on the job away, teaching three year olds to sing "Jesus Loves Me," and still up and nursing everybody else in the family who is down with the flu.

You can find mothers championing causes that affect their families, making wrongs right, kissing the hurts away, struggling to understand this new math, gently changing her husband's mind about how to deal with a wayward child, staring daggers at the football referee who just called her child off-sides, baking cupcakes for the school festival, praying on her knees, suspending privileges, granting back privileges, pushing violin practice, and then one day sitting in the mother's place on a pew as her little child is being married.

You can define a mother as a lady with happiness expressed with tears in her eyes, love with the paddle firmly in hand, joy watching dad and the kids devour warm chocolate chip cookies and cold milk. She will sacrifice by eating the wings and leaving the drumstick and breast. She exercises forethought and planning by stashing something away for college, faithfully teaching a Sunday school class or singing in the choir, bringing another hot-dish to another church supper, making sure the missions pledge is paid on time, and is always ready to listen to her child.

Being a mother is such a special and demanding task that God only trusted females to do it! There is no other life experience which can be so costly, rewarding, aging, taxing, and exciting as being a MOTHER!

But in spite of the above . . . today, lots of people, men and women, are concerned about WHO they are, what they are to be, what they are to do.

Dr. James Dobson said that he thinks "feminism developed in this country, especially in some of its more militant forms because men were not fulfilling the role that they were called to in the home. Neither were men appreciating women for the important role they are playing."

Dr. Paul Tournier points out that "our society has been shaped since the Renaissance by scientific rationalism, by an approach that focuses so totally on material things and on human achievement that we have forgotten the importance of relationships, of human emotion, and of the needs of people."

Today, all of us are one day closer to our time of death! When faced with this fact, what is really important? Titles? Influence? Power? Achievements? Money? Position?

None of these are that important. What really matters in that moment of final reality is our personal relationships. That's exactly what women are the very best at: RELATIONSHIPS! This world is desperately in need of seeing and being a part of the kinds of relationships built on this kind of love. Today, our society desperately needs the influence and actions of godly Christian women that reaches even beyond our homes.

If the women of America don't stand up against such things as exploitation in pornography and abortion and injustices of all kinds . . . who will? If the women of a nation lose their virtue, the nation will lose everything, eventually.

*As Christian women learn WHO they really are . . . they will respond to God as intercessors in prayer!

*As Christian women learn WHO they are . . . they will be used as the instruments of healing and peace. Women are the fixers of the world, able to mend and bring broken relationships back together! I have often wondered if the world would be in the mess it's in if women had equal positions of leadership.

*As Christian women learn WHO they are . . . they will take their place as key players in God's plan for this present age! Your role is a crucial one!

I remind you once more that in the total plan of God, as expressed in the writings of Paul, "There is neither Jew nor Greek, slave nor free, MALE NOR FEMALE, for YOU ARE ALL ONE IN CHRIST JESUS" (Gal. 3:28).

WHO are you? You have been set free from any bondage placed upon you because of your social status, economic status, or gender status! Together we are one!

It's my hope that all women will begin to understand WHO they are and HOW God wants to use them! It's my further hope that Christian MEN will begin to look at women through new eyes, through the eyes of God who made us and fashioned us and fashioned women for His plans and His purposes!

Dee Jepson who served as Special Assistant to the President for Public Liaison to women's organizations during the President Reagan era, relates the following: "One day I was privileged to sit at a table next to Mother Teresa of Calcutta. I had long admired her and her work with the destitute and dying in Calcutta and throughout the world. The Capital Hill luncheon in honor of Mother Teresa was held in the ornately decorated Senate caucus room in the Russell Building. As she entered, she seemed dwarfed by the enormity of the room. She was even tinier than I had expected. As she walked into the room, clad in a simple blue and white habit, I saw some of the strongest leaders in the world rise to their feet and applaud her with tears in their eyes. They were honored simply to be in her presence.

"Here was a woman who obviously had tremendous power. She possessed more power than those who walked the marble halls of Congress. She had more power than I had seen in this city of power. How had she done this? I asked myself. She owned nothing, never shook her fist in anger for her rights, and never asked for anything for herself. Instead, she had reached down into the gutter and raised up and loved those of the world whom the world called unlovable. And she had done it simply because the poor were created by God and she loves and serves.

"All of us that day were humbled in her presence because we knew how full of ourselves we were. God in His wisdom had once again used the simple to confound the wise. He had elevated this little woman to a place of international recognition and honor!"

Ma'am, on your behalf, as well as on the behalf of all of your sisters, my prayer is that our world, our families, our men, will learn to "Give you [her] the reward you [she] have [has] earned, and let your [her] works bring you [her] praise at the city gate" (Prov. 31:31)!

TODAY'S BIBLE READING: Proverbs 31:10-31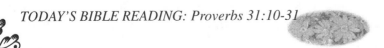

7.
EXTRAVAGANT LOVE

Wayne Rouse of Hastings, Nebraska, writes the following: "The most sobering account of extravagant love that I know, is demonstrated by a friend of my wife, Alice Rangal. Alice grew up with my wife in Cozad, Nebraska. Her mother and grandmother had a reputation for being 'the worst of the worst.' They were known for drinking and sleeping around, and they made life miserable for Alice and her brothers and sisters.

"One afternoon, while in a drunken state, her mother and grandmother had all the kids in the car, and they stalled the car on the railroad tracks. Off in the distance a Union Pacific freight train blew its whistle, and Alice could see the train racing toward them. When Alice realized that her mother and grandmother were too drunk to understand the danger they were in, she began to get her brothers and sisters out of the car. As she was pulling both of them to safety, the train hit the car at 60 miles an hour.

"Alice's extravagant love saved her family's life, but cost her own. As the train smashed into their car, Alice was too close and was decapitated."[5]

Love . . . extravagant love, is the special ingredient to all of life, but especially so in the life of a mother. Where does love originate? Where does love come from? There is only one source: "God is love!" The Bible is the ultimate authority on love. Here is the command to all of us as given by Jesus Christ: "A new command I give you: LOVE ONE AN-OTHER. As I have loved you, so you must love one another. By this all men will know that you are my disciples, if you love one another" (John 13:34-35). Powerful!

The world has a right to see among all who are true believers a kind of love that cuts across language, nationality, age, color of skin, levels of education, economics, dress, forms of worship, and gender. If it doesn't see this, how will they know we are real disciples? Society is looking for more than correct answers. They will judge our love on the basis of something they can see, hear, and observe. We can talk about it, think about it . . . but how can we really make it a seeable, visible, observable love?

First: THIS MEANS I ASK FORGIVENESS. How simple! It's almost a let-down in its simplicity. The only path I know to re-building broken relationships between parent and child, wife and husband, or between anybody and myself is through forgiveness. If I'm not willing to say "I'm sorry, will you please forgive me?" when I have wronged another, I don't even begin to know the meaning of love.

The world looks at us with our splits, broken homes, hurting marriages, lawsuits, our anger against each other, and just shrugs thinking that we are no different than they are. It's our sharp tongues and lack of love that bothers people of this world . . . not our statements of differences.

Second: THERE MUST ALSO BE AN OPEN, HONEST ACT OF FORGIVENESS. This goes beyond asking forgiveness. It's harder when I must do the forgiving! The world is looking for this forgiving spirit at work among us. And this can be outrageously costly! Who wants to cut the perpetrator free from their transgression and let him go free?!

How often have you expressed, "Forgive us our trespasses, as we forgive those who trespass against us"? Few among us seem likely to connect our own lack of reality in relationship with God with our lack of forgiveness to others.

Our love may not be perfect . . . but it must be substantial enough for the world to be able to observe our honest offering of forgiveness or it doesn't fit into the real concept of love.

Third: THERE MUST BE A DEMONSTRATION OF COSTLY LOVE. It's more than raising a banner over us proclaiming our love. It's an action of love that demonstrates love. We cannot sing about our love for God and then turn around and commit an action considered not to be loving. Our words and our actions must be congruent or we have no validity. You don't go around forcing this kind of action . . . but when the opportunity arises, like Alice in our story, you do what is needed.

Fourth: NEVER FORGET THE STANDARD. Do you want people around you to believe that a relationship with God is real? Would you like your family, friends, relatives, and neighbors to know that you are a true disciple, a real follower of this God of love? Never forget the command! If you should fail . . . refer once more to the first and second concepts as written above. If we mess up . . . fess up and make it right and go on! Love and the unity it attests to is "the mark" Jesus Christ gave to us to wear before the world. This is the only way the world will know that we are a true follower!

Here's how this thing of costly, extravagant love worked out in the life of a lady who was a member of the church my father pastored in Mansfield, Ohio. She had been widowed, losing her husband in an industrial accident, and now hers was the full responsibility to raise their three little children. This took place during tough times, the late 1930s.

The only way she could earn enough to keep body and soul together was to take in washing and ironing. One day as she was washing and hanging out the clothes to dry (it had rained earlier in the day but now the sun was out), she put a load of whites on the lines and went back down into her basement to carry out another load. Her next door neighbor, a man who could have easily qualified for the title of "world's meanest man," for spite, came across the yard with his hunting knife in hand and cut all her clotheslines to drop the white wash into the mud of the wet ground.

When she came out with the next basketfull, she immediately saw what had been done and knew immediately who had done it! She dropped her basket and sat on the top back step and just cried. After her cry, she picked up the dirty wash and went back to the basement to do that load all over again. She returned upstairs and repaired the lines as best she could, readying them for the re-washed load. As she worked, bitterness was growing in her and she was planning and plotting revenge. It was so sweet she could almost taste it . . . the things she would do in retaliation.

She continued with the washing and hanging out of the wash when . . . suddenly, she was impressed with the thought that this was not the time for revenge but an opportunity to show love and forgiveness. She argued with herself and with the Lord! NO! But that inner urging was persistent . . . make an investment of love . . . go the second mile . . . forgive. But how?

She began to pray and asked the Lord to forgive her of her hatred and immediately thought of making her specialty . . . homemade lemon pie with meringue on top! NO! How could she? Impossible! Too costly! The argument raged inside.

Finally, she gave in and baked the pie. While it was still warm, she took it next door, knocked , and when he appeared presented the pie with a smile and said, graciously, "I forgive you."

He didn't know what to say . . . extravagant love instead of retaliation! He broke and tears began to roll down his cheeks. He was speechless. He motioned her to sit on one of the porch chairs as he set the pie on a nearby stand. He asked her how she could do such a thing in return for his meanness. She then was able to share simply with him that she was a disciple, a discipled follower of Jesus Christ who loved him no matter how mean he was. She offered to pray with him and for him. Right then and there, he accepted Jesus Christ as his own personal Lord and Saviour.

Oh, yes, there is one more detail. This world's meanest man was a bachelor living alone following the death of his mother. Well to make the long story even a bit longer . . . romance blossomed and before the year was over, they married and have lived happily together ever after!

Now I can't guarantee that you will get this kind of a result . . . but you are to go and do likewise! Costly, extravagant love offered to all who offend!

TODAY'S BIBLE READING: John 13:31-14:31

8.
A BETTER FRIEND

Early in 1995, on a rainy, cold February day, a limousine traveling down the New Jersey expressway pulled off to the side of the road with a flat tire. The limo driver dutifully got out to change the tire, only to discover that the spare tire was also flat. Before the uniformed driver could summon a road service, a man in a pickup truck pulled up behind the limo, stopped, got out, and offered to help. Among the equipment in the back of his truck was an air tank.

The truck driver quickly fixed the flat, aired it up, and placed it back on the limo. As the job was finished, the rear window slid down and the truck driver was surprised to see Donald Trump sitting inside. "This was so very nice of you to stop and help," Trump said. "What can I do to thank you?"

The man thought for a moment and said, "Tomorrow is Valentine's Day. My wife would really get a kick out of receiving a dozen roses from you." Trump agreed, got the name and address and drove off with the fixed flat in his limo.

The next day, a messenger arrived at the house with a long box. When the surprised wife opened the box she found two dozen red roses and a note which read: "Happy Valentine's Day from a friend of your husband. (signed) Donald Trump." And at the bottom there was a P.S. "Thanks for helping us out. By the way, I paid off your home mortgage."[6]

Yes, that is a true story! Think of it! Just to have one's house mortgage paid off would be a wonderful, tremendous gift. Even to think of the possibility brings a smile to the face. What a delightful surprise.

But there's an even more exciting story of canceling a debt. Jesus Christ came to live among people so He could die for all of us. In His atonement, sacrifice, the price was paid so we could go debt-free, free of our guilt and sin! In this price is included freedom from the bondage which a lifestyle of sin has placed upon us. Jesus paid for all of your sins . . . past, present, and future! Now that's worth a celebration. There's more relief here than having all our financial debts paid.

When we look at life . . . what does really matter? What really counts in life? Get to the essence of the matter, what matters? It's a question that sort of hangs in the air. Don't give us any more religious stuff . . . we really want to know.

What does really matter?

Do we think about the 23rd Psalm? "The Lord is my shepherd. . . . " Important, but still, is it the meat of the question before us? The Bible can be read cover to cover and you discover a whole lot of "do's and don't's" and "should's and shouldn't's" . . . but again, come to the essential.

Would it be found in John 3:16? "For God so loved this world. . . ."

Maybe I'm assuming too much. Perhaps you have never really wrestled with this issue before. Maybe you have gone through the motions . . . prayers seem to accomplish nothing, goals don't make sense, living the Christian life is sort of nothing more than ups and downs.

Is this all there is to it?

Sunday finds you in church . . . worship songs . . . faithful in giving tithes and offerings . . . nice faces all cleaned up in Sunday best . . . choirs . . . Bibles. . . .

I still remember the first time I was asked that question. Claudia was the questioner, seated across our kitchen table in the parsonage, humble surroundings in the back of the church which was adjacent to Mankato State College campus. She was a student, a young lady who had been born with a silver spoon in her mouth, privileged, but now on a quest for truth. "What really matters?" she had asked. I responded with the usual. I was younger and had to have an answer to all such questions. I had answered, but all the canned responses seemed to fall a little bit short.

Now as I reflect, I have an answer. Here's what I would share with Claudia today.

Think about the words written by the apostle Paul:

> For what I received I passed on to you as *of FIRST IMPORTANCE:* that Christ died for our sins according to the Scriptures (1 Cor. 15:3; italics mine).

"First importance" and there it is! He said it for Claudia and for all of us! Read on:

That he was buried, that he was raised on the third day according to the Scriptures, and that he appeared to Peter, and then to the Twelve (1 Cor. 15:4).

It's so simple we tend to overlook it. This is the essence, this is the meat, this is what really matters. Jesus was killed, buried, and resurrected. The Cross was the instrument. It can be erected at the very crossroads of the time-line of all of human history. The pathos and tragedy calls all of us. Because of its absurdity, cynics stumble over it. History has gold-plated it, attempted to burn it, worn it on a chain, trashed it, idolized it, despised it. Time has passed and history has been made and rewritten . . . but still the Cross remains, it cannot be ignored!

No one can ignore it. The Man who was crucified on it claimed to be God, claimed to be the one who could conquer death! It's pretty sobering when you think about it . . . if it is true, it is the hinge upon which all history must swing. If it is not true, then it is the most colossal hoax in all of history. And that's why it matters.

That is exactly why the Cross is what matters! Any serious thinking person looking at any of the claims of Christ or Christianity or what life is all about must either accept or reject the cross. Here the sacrifice was made which allows us to have received the gift that cancels all of our debt of sin!

No wonder Jesus is called the "Saviour"!

He is the very best friend any woman could ever have!

TODAY'S BIBLE READING: I Corinthians 15:1-58

9.
THE FINAL GOODBYE

She was special. She was one of those wonderful, grand old saints who was there every time the church doors were open . . . never any excuses. Salt of the earth, faithful. During the weekdays, she busied herself with Christian duties and simple dedication. She had been a widow for more than a decade. She had been dying for months and she was fully prepared to do so. The Rev. Gene Rutland, her pastor, stopped by quite often to visit. He was understandably puzzled to receive her message requesting a special visit from her pastor.

Pastor Rutland called on her that very evening. She was in excellent spirits. "Gene," she said, "we both know that this can't go on much longer. When I die, I want you to promise me that you will carry out a special request."

"Of course," Pastor Rutland promised her.

She reinforced the promise, "Gene, you do it. I'm sure my kids wouldn't do it." Again he assured her.

"When the casket is opened at the funeral," she explained, "and all my friends come by for a last look, I want them to see me ready to be buried with a table fork in my right hand." Rutland must have looked puzzled by her request, but she continued, "I want you to tell the congregation. You know what it means when they clear the dishes from a big meal and someone says, 'keep your fork.' You know that something good is coming . . . maybe a piece of apple pie with cheese on it or a big slab of chocolate cake."

She concluded, "Keep your fork, means something good is coming. Gene, I want to be buried with a dessert fork in my hand. It will be my way of saying, 'The best is yet to come.' "

Four days later, she was buried with a fork in her hand just as she had requested. Everyone who saw her in the casket saw her final witness. For her, death was not a disaster. It was a dessert! [7]

When you read the Bible, if you think as you read, you are struck by the many challenges written that go against human nature. One of these reads, "And everyone who has left houses or brothers or sisters or father or mother or children or fields for my sake will receive a hundred times as much and will inherit eternal life" (Matt. 19:29).

That part about leaving houses and lands is understood . . . but what about saying a final goodbye to family members? Do I have to be willing to leave people I love? That seems to be more like a final act of sacrifice. How much more sacrificial can it be?

"Dear woman, here is your son," and to the disciple, "Here is your mother" (John 19:26).

Let's take another look at this mother, Mary. It's not the Mary that artists have given us, this Mary at the Cross must have had hair turning gray at the temples. Time has caused wrinkles to replace the youthful skin of the virgin. Hands are now callused. Perhaps she is a bit stooped or bent over. Life was not easy for women in those days. She had raised a whole houseful of kids. But now . . . she stands and watches the crucifixion of her first-born son.

What do you suppose are the memories going through her mind as she watches His torture? Does she think about the donkey ride to Bethlehem? Perhaps about that first bed made in a manger holding hay for cattle? Dinner times? Carpentry apprenticeship? Table-time laughter?

Maybe it was that morning when He came in from the carpenter shop for the last time . . . the look in His eyes conveyed something she'd never seen before. He was direct. Slowly He peeled off His apron, dusted off His hands. Held her close, said a goodbye, and left. He had heard that his cousin John was now preaching in the wilderness. They both knew some things would be changed and would never be the same again. In that last parting look they shared a special secret which may have been too painful for either of them to have expressed aloud.

Had Mary already bid a final farewell to her own husband? I believe so, because none of the Gospel writers ever talk about Joseph. She had been a widow, then. Jesus was the eldest and into His care she had been thrust. Mary learned again the heartache of saying goodbye.

From that parting she was to follow and love her son from a ways off, in the distance, at the edge of the crowd, sharing Him at a wedding. Perhaps she had been there to hear Him say, "Anyone who has left . . . mother . . . for my sake. . . ."

Mary was not the first Bible person to be asked to say goodbye to someone deeply loved for the sake of the kingdom. Hannah sent away her firstborn son so he could serve in the temple. Timothy's mother and grandmother must have bid him goodbye so he could travel with Paul. Elizabeth, too, said her final farewell to her own son who was to prepare the way for Mary's son. The Bible is full of goodbyes and farewell tears.

It seems as though that word "goodbye" is wrapped up in much of a Christian's vocabulary. Missionaries know it too well . . . airports, luggage, hugs, tears, tickets, tight throats, and always, "Write me!"

Why would God put people through such agony? Why would you be given a family only to later have to leave them? What kind of a God would do such things that hurt so much?

Because this God knows that the deepest kinds of love are built on common sacrifice. Love that is built on romance and passion needs more.

Because God knows that in this life we are only pilgrims. Eternity is so close for all of us. So a "goodbye" here in reality is a "see you tomorrow in eternity."

Life is short and life is not fair! But it's long enough so that you can prepare for the day and time when you will be saying a final goodbye.

Will you say goodbye with a dessert fork in your hand? It all depends on how you have lived life while you are getting ready for your final goodbye!

TODAY'S BIBLE READING: John 19:1-42

10.
ONE WHO INFLUENCED MY LIFE

One last figure towers above all others who have influenced my life: My mother, known as "Granny Brand." I say it kindly and in love, but in old age my mother had little of physical beauty left in her. She had been a classic beauty as a young woman . . . I have photographs to prove it . . . but not in old age. The rugged conditions in India, combined with crippling falls and her battle with typhoid, dysentery, and malaria had made her a thin, hunched-over old woman. Years of exposure to wind and sun had toughened her facial skin into leather and furrowed it with wrinkles as deep and extensive as any I have seen on a human face. She knew better than anyone that her physical appearance had long since failed her . . . for this reason she adamantly refused to keep a mirror in her house.

At the age of 75, while working in the mountains of South India, my mother fell and broke her hip. She lay all night on the floor in pain until a workman found her the next morning. Four men carried her on a string-and-wood cot down the mountain path and put her in a jeep for an agonizing 150-mile ride over rutted roads. (She had made this trip before, after a headfirst fall off a horse on a rocky mountain path, and already had experienced some paralysis below her knees.)

I scheduled a visit to my mother's mud-walled home in order to persuade her to retire. By then she could walk only with the aid of two bamboo canes taller than she was, planting the canes and lifting her legs high with each painful step to keep her paralyzed feet from dragging. Yet she continued to travel on horseback and camp in the outlying villages in order to preach the gospel and treat sicknesses and pull the decayed teeth of the villagers.

I came with compelling arguments for her retirement. It was not safe for her to go on living alone in such a remote place with good help a day's journey away. With her faulty sense of balance and paralyzed legs she presented a constant medical hazard. Already she had endured fractures of vertebrae and ribs, pressure on her spinal nerve roots, a brain concussion, a fractured femur, and severe infection of her hand. "Even the best of people do sometimes retire when they reach their seventies," I said with a smile. "Why not come to Vellore and live near us?"

Granny threw off my arguments like so much nonsense and shot back a reprimand. Who would continue the work? There was no one else in the entire mountain range to preach, to bind up wounds, and to pull teeth. "In any case," she concluded, "what is the use of preserving my old body if it is not going to be used where God needs me?"

And so she stayed. Eighteen years later, at the age of 93, she reluctantly gave up sitting on her pony because she was falling all too frequently. Devoted Indian villagers began bearing her on a hammock from town to town. After two more years of mission work, she finally died at age 95. She was buried, at her request, in a simple, well-used sheet laid in the ground . . . no coffin. She abhorred the notion of wasting precious wood on coffins. Also, she liked the symbolism of returning her physical body to its original humus even as her spirit was set free.

One of my last and strongest memories of my mother is set in a village in the mountains she loved, perhaps the last time I saw her in her own environment. She is sitting on a low stone wall that circles the village, with people pressing in from all sides. They are listening to all she has to say about Jesus. Heads are nodding, and deep, searching questions come from the crowd. Granny's own eyes are shining, and standing beside her I can see what she must be seeing through failing eyes: intent faces gazing with absolute trust and affection on one they have grown to love.

I know that even with my relative youth and strength and all my specialized knowledge about health and agricultural techniques, I could never command that kind of devotion and love from these people. They are looking at a wrinkled old face, but somehow her shrunken tissues have become transparent and she is all lambent spirit. To them, she is beautiful. Granny Brand had no need for a mirror made of glass and polished chromium; she had the incandescent face of thousands of Indian villagers. Her worn-out physical image did nothing but enhance the image of God beaming through her like a beacon.[8]

TODAY'S BIBLE READING:
1 Corinthians 12:12–13:13

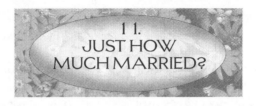

11.
JUST HOW MUCH MARRIED?

Bob had not been feeling too well of late, so he made an appointment with the family doctor at the local clinic. On the appointed day, after making sure the kids would have a sitter present when they came home from school, he and his wife, Donna, drove to the clinic. Later that afternoon, after a whole battery of tests and exams, their family practitioner said, "Bob, if you don't mind, I'd like to talk to Donna while you get dressed. We'll wait for you in my office."

Donna sat across the desk, while the doctor explained, "Donna, your husband has a rare and potentially terminal disease. He is suffering from a potentially fatal stress-related disorder. You will need to create a totally stress-free environment for your husband if he is to survive." He paused for the impact of that news to sink into her head.

Then he continued, "Donna, I know you have a good career . . . but you must quit your job and become a stay-at-home wife. You'll need to get up at least a half an hour earlier each morning, shower, and put on a fresh outfit. Fix your hair and put on your make-up. Prepare a nutritious, healthy breakfast. I'll give you his special diet requirements. The emphasis for breakfasts will be on fresh fruits and whole grains. You will do this so that when he has showered and dressed he can sit down to a ready breakfast, remember no stress, no conversation to upset him as the day starts. Then send your husband off to work with a big hug and a kiss. Smile and wish him a good day."

Donna is busy taking notes while the doctor continues, "As soon as he leaves the house, put on your work clothes and clean and scrub the house from top to bottom. Remove any possible allergic or pathogenic source of stress. This is important. About an hour before lunch, shower and get ready for your husband to come home for lunch, less stress than those business lunches, you know. Prepare him a light, high protein lunch with emphasis again on fresh fruits, but this meal with salads. Send him back to work with another kiss and spend your afternoon thoroughly preparing your house for his homecoming in the afternoon."

He pauses for effect and goes on, "Meet him at the door when he comes home for dinner, again, freshly showered, make-up applied, and dressed. Give him a big kiss and lead him to his favorite chair. Give him a refreshing fruit-cooler type of drink. Bring the newspaper and the TV remote. Tell him to relax while you finish preparing the evening meal. Make sure the kids are on the quiet side and don't bother him with their homework. Make sure the evening menu does include one or more of his very favorite dishes. After dinner, encourage him to relax while you tidy up the kitchen and lay out his pajamas and draw his hot bath. Be attentive to his every need during the evening. And of course, be just as romantic as you possibly can be. Remember, his health and life is at stake."

On the ride home, Bob anxiously asked, "Donna, what did the doctor tell you?"

Donna was quiet for a long time as she prepared her answer, then finally, she said, "He said you're going to die."

Maybe you just needed to laugh today, wife! Now you've got a good story to share. But don't begin with, "Here's a funny story I read the other day. . . ." If you tell someone it will be funny, it might not be, so just tell it!

Some of God's choicest servants have been happy, joyful people. Take Oswald Chambers, as an example. He is the man behind one of the best devotionals ever written, *My Utmost for His Highest*, and known as a person with a rollicking sense of humor. After meeting Oswald for the first time, one serious-minded young man said, "I was shocked at what I then considered his undue levity. He was the most irreverent Reverend I had ever met!"

The well-known Charles Spurgeon of much writing and many commentaries was rebuked by a lady in his congregation for too much humor in his preaching, to which he replied, "Madam, you should give me a medal for holding it back as much as I do."

To be joyful is an attitude, a decision, and a discipline. To laugh is to chuckle, giggle, roar, chortle, guffaw, snicker, titter, cackle, roll in the aisle, howl, be joyful, make merry, be mirthful, belly laugh, and to split one's side! Are you aware that the word "rejoice" appears at least 248 times in the Bible!? Did you also know that the words "joy, joyful, joyfully" in some form appears some 200 times? The word "laugh" is penned some 40 times in the Bible.

Let's remind ourselves of Proverbs 17:22 real often: "A cheerful heart is good medicine, but a crushed spirit dries up the bones" (NIV). Another translation goes like this, "A rejoicing heart doeth good to the body" (YLT). The Knox translation reads: "A cheerful heart makes a quick recovery."

Laughter and joyfulness are first attitudes. Attitudes are formed by convictions. Christians are people who have developed or are developing strong convictions as to who they are, where they are going, who God is, what His love is about, that His word gives us life direction, and his joy builds inner strength for life and living. These kinds of people have healthier, more joyful attitudes toward life than those who do not have such deep-seated convictions.

Laughter is an expression of joy flowing, happiness showing, countenance glowing, kind of an attitude toward life! Can you imagine God laughing? Here it is from Psalm 2:4: "The One enthroned in heaven laughs."

God loves joyful people and it appears that He loves to give joy to His people. Listen, "And on that day they offered great sacrifices, rejoicing because God had given them great joy. The women and children also rejoiced. The sound of rejoicing in Jerusalem could be heard far away" (Neh. 12:43). That must have been quite a party! I just want to call your attention once more to the line that indicates the source of their "rejoicing because GOD HAD GIVEN THEM GREAT JOY!"

Have you noticed that most people who are happy rarely are the richest, or most beautiful, or most talented? Happy, joyful people, do not depend upon externals in order to be happy! Happy people are adaptable, flexible, glad to be alive, have learned how to savor life, adjust, and enjoy! They are giving, focused outward, aware, compassionate, loving, and victorious.

People who consistently are joyful and full of laughter do so in spite of, seldom because of, anything! If God is God, then joy and laughter fits life! To be joyful is a choice!

Here is one powerful resolution: "Though the fig tree does not bud and there are no grapes on the vines, though the olive crop fails and the field produce no food, though there are no sheep in the pen and no cattle in the stalls, YET I WILL REJOICE IN THE LORD, I WILL BE JOYFUL IN GOD MY SAVIOR" (Hab. 3:17-18, caps are mine)!

 TODAY'S BIBLE READING:
Nehemiah 8:1-18

12.
THIEVES WHO ROB YOUR JOY

The Rev. William Goodin writes: "My first really glorious mistake happened at the first of our new pastorate. One of the local hospitals called the office and said that one of our members had been admitted to their hospital. I asked for directions. When I arrived, the patient was not in her hospital bed, so I left a note and went back to my unpacking. Since she was in a bed in the maternity ward of the hospital, I had a 'motherhood prayer' for her the next day, Sunday.

"What I didn't know was that there was a flu epidemic in the city at the time and the lady had been placed in the only empty bed available. She was 87 years old, a great-grandmother, and I prayed for her and her new baby, publicly, in my pastoral prayer. No one remembers who preached that day, nor what was said. But everyone remembered my prayer! The giggles lasted all the way through the sermon. . . . I just knew it was going to be a long and interesting year."[9]

People who have trusted in Jesus Christ as their personal Lord and Saviour also have the opportunity to experience "fullness of joy" according to Psalm 16:11. Yet . . . too few Christians take advantage of this privilege. Too many are living under a cloud of disappointment when they could be walking in the sunshine of joy. Mother . . . what has robbed you of your joy?

We live in a world where lots of thieves are at work. In order to protect our material goods and our own persons, most of us take preventive measures and make preparations against any possible losses. Yet in the spiritual sense, we casually allow any number of thieves to rob us of our joy to live in defeat and under a cloud. How many of these thieves have been at work in your life?

CIRCUMSTANCES: Let's be honest here . . . how many of you will own up to the fact that we feel happier when things are going our way? Right? Right!

Peggy, who is seven years old, was entertaining her girl friend and she said this when her father arrived home from work: "Daddy must have had an easy day at the office, he didn't squeal the tires when he pulled into the driveway and he didn't slam the door and he even gave my mother a kiss."

When you think of circumstances . . . have you considered just how few of those circumstances of life are really under your control? Can you control the weather? Traffic? Permanents that turn out frizzy? Ovens that go on the blink when company is about to descend? The next election?

PEOPLE: A high-schooler, who shall remain unnamed, jumped off the school bus, slammed her way through the front door, marched defiantly to her room, slinging books, jacket, and back-pack . . . slammed the bedroom door . . . all the time muttering under her breath, louder each time she said it: "People, PEOple, peoPLE, PEOPLE!"

After a discreet pause, her mother softly went to the bedroom door, knocked softly, and asked, "May I come in?"
From inside came back, "NO!"
She asked again, "Honey, may I come in?"
This time, louder, from inside, "NO!!"
She asked, "Why can't I come in?"
Her answer, "Because you are a people!"

Lots of us have lost our joy because of people . . . because of what they say, what they are, what they do! Oh, by the way, have you ever caused somebody else to lose their joy because of what you said, what you are, or what you did? OUCH! Well, it works both ways.

We must live, work, parent, play, shop, and worship with others. It's impossible to be isolated from people. But to complicate things further . . . we are commissioned to be the salt of the earth and the light of this world. And sometimes the light grows dim and the salt becomes tasteless because of others. So our problem boils down the question: Is it possible for you to have joy in spite of people?

THINGS: A wealthy family was moving into their country estate and their Quaker neighbor, who believed in the simplicity of life, was watching the activities carefully . . . tables, chairs, couches, bric-abrac, and the vast amounts of furniture that was being carried into the house. Finally, the Quaker said to the incoming man of the estate: "Neighbor, if thou dost need anything, come to see me and I will tell thee how to get along without it."

Too many people think that joy comes from the things they might possess. When I get that new kitchen, then I'll be happy! When that new set of dishes is mine, then I'll be happy! When I have my first car, then I'll be happy!

Just think of the maintenance required by the things we own. Think of the first leak in the roof of that new house. Think of the times you will be dusting, cleaning, mowing, clipping, polishing, insuring, maintaining, and painting it! Jesus said, "Watch out! Be on your guard against all kinds of greed . . . life does not consist in the abundance of . . . possessions" (Luke 12:15).

WORRY: Worry is an inside job and may be the worst thief of all. You can purchase sleep at the drugstore, but you can't purchase rest or peace. Worry is kind of like sitting in a rocking chair . . . something to do, but no place to go. Jesus pointed out to all of us how useless it is to worry: "Who of you by worrying can add a single hour to your life?" (Matt. 6:27). Not a one of us can do that! But by worrying it is possible to subtract hours from your life.

SELF-PITY: There are probably few mothers who have not at some time done battle with this thief. It's the result of being inward-focused rather than outward or upward-focused.

Self-pity plagued the people of Israel. When faced with a problem they wished they had either died in the wilderness or still lived in bondage in Egypt. And all of that generation eventually did die in the wilderness because self-pity was one of the thieves that robbed them of their faith, that robbed them of their hope which in turn took away all their joy at being set free from the Egyptian slavery.

ATTITUDE: Yes, this is important. Why? In reality, your attitude is the only thing over which you have complete control. Attitude sets the pace for just about everything you think, say, or do. The philosopher Will James said: "The greatest discovery of the 20th century is that a person can change her (his) life by changing her (his) thoughts."

The Bible warns: "Above all else, guard your heart [mind], for it is the wellspring of life" (Prov. 4:23). From the King James translation this verse reads: "Keep thy heart with all diligence; for out of it are the issues of life."

Some of us are in drastic need of a check-up from the neck-up!

GRIEF: Grief takes all kinds of disguises, suddenly, unexpectedly, agonizingly long. Grief hurts! But grief heals if we allow time and the joy of the Lord to sustain us. Read these next verses carefully. . . .

"Each heart knows its own bitterness, and no one else can share its joy" (Prov. 14:10).

"Even in laughter the heart may ache, and joy may end in grief" (Prov. 14:13).

"Weeping may remain for a night, but rejoicing comes in the morning" (Ps. 30:5).

This world is filled with two kinds of people, two kinds of Christians: People who choose joy and people who don't.

The people who choose joy, choose it no matter what day of the week it may be . . . people who choose joy choose it no matter how young or old they may be . . . people who choose joy no matter what level of pain they may be experiencing are the people who choose to live, really live!

People who choose joy will find it a never-ending source of strength!

This thing called JOY depends on knowing who you are in relationship to the Lord who is our ultimate source of strength and JOY!

TODAY'S BIBLE READING: Psalm 30:1-12

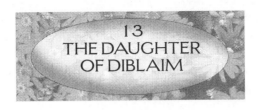

The town gossips were at it again, "Can you believe it? The prophet is marrying one of our town prostitutes!" This strange story begins with the scandal-mongers in Israel grinding out their dreadful story. It is the pitiful story of rejected love, a squandered life spent seeking illicit pleasures among the playboy set of the area. Can such news be true? What kind of a scandal is this upon the life and ministry of the prophet?

We are engaged in one of the strangest stories in all of the Bible. It's a story that at first seems repulsive, yet through this tragic object lesson God teaches all of us about His mercy. Here is a story of forgiving love. Because it's set in the confines of human experience, we can catch a glimpse of something more than the story of two people.

God tells the prophet Hosea, "Go, take to yourself an adulterous wife and children of unfaithfulness" (Hos. 1:2). My first reaction would be, "God, do You know what You are asking?" After Hosea got over the initial shock, "he married Gomer daughter of Diblaim, and she conceived and bore him a son" (Hos. 1:3).

Prostitution is the oldest of con games. Is there hope for the hustler? Does God know what He's doing? A most unusual command. He's asking his faithful prophet to take a wife from off the street. This strumpet will surely harm the reputation of a man of God. The whole idea of a prophet and a harlot is preposterous . . . but it happened! Gomer was a cool call girl, one ruthless woman in a lucrative racket. Selling her body had been her means of financial support. Matrimony would not reform Gomer overnight. This marriage was to be a real life parable lived out for all to see.

Despite Gomer's questionable background the prophet finds happiness with his bride. There begins to spring up a tender love for this woman he has plucked from the hotbed of vice. Love binds them together. They parent a son, then a daughter, then another son, three kids in all. The woman who once sold herself now finds security and happiness as the wife of the prophet. This prophet and his promiscuous wife and her kids lived together for a time under the same roof and became an object lesson which was to illustrate God's dealings with a wayward people.

Gomer values her new life, lightly. A restlessness begins to grow in her. She turns from the faithful and unselfish love of a man of God to the sensual and faithless lust of the paramours of Israel. Eager to make the most of her life, she squanders her God-given powers for the gratification of pleasure.

She returns to the street . . . but the price is not cheap. She leaves the side of Hosea to taste once again the pleasures of the world. This world then betrays her until at last she finds herself at the very bottom rung of humanity. She's helpless, betrayed, a harlot — now chained and held for auction in a Jewish slave market!

But it seems that true love never dies. Here the story begins to show the everlasting love of God in human experience. Hosea's heart has been broken. There have been endless nights of pain, grief, and heaviness. He has gathered his three kids about him, to comfort them, as he agonizingly watches her descent into the total blackness of the night. How many nights had Jezreel, Loruhamah, and LoAmmi cried themselves to sleep waiting for their mommy to return home?

Then there was the day Hosea read the notice posted for the next slave auction. Gomer's name was listed!

That morning finally arrives. A woman's trembling form shivers in the cold air as the first rays of light penetrate the blackness of what had seemed to her the longest night she had spent on earth. She stands up . . . she stretches which brings sudden awareness to her. This is the day . . . Gomer shudders . . . to be sold at a slave auction!

The rooster crows . . . the prophet awakens. Excitement pulses through his veins as he contemplates the challenge of this day. He has waited long. He gets the kids up and ready for the day, then leaves them in the care of a neighbor.

Business of the day begins as any other. Little notice is taken of Hosea as he wends his way toward the market place where a large and raucous crowd has gathered to watch or take part in the monthly auction of human slaves. They hoot and howl as slaves are presented and bidders vie. It's the regular sale of human souls. The bidding rises and falls, slaves change owners as though they were cattle.

At length a female slave appears, more downcast than the rest. Gone is the bloom of youth, she cringes at her exposure to the crowd. A smile crosses the auctioneer's face as he cries out in a mocking voice, "Hear ye, hear ye, men of Israel! What will you bid for a prophet's wife?" Laughter breaks forth, the mob jeers, the bids begin to rise.

A new awareness grips the crowd. Suddenly they become conscious of a strange voice bidding with the rest. A voice never before heard at this auction. The laughter begins to die as the people turn to recognize Hosea the prophet . . . bidding for this most wretched of all slaves!

"Going once, going twice. . . ."

One final bidder, in a voice that betrays the emotion of the moment. The crowd remains silent, watching, listening, "Fifteen shekels of silver, one homer, and a lethek of barley!"

"Going and gone! SOLD to the prophet!"

The gathered crowd watches in astonishment. Hosea places the barley and silver on the table. Gomer's chains are removed. He throws a shawl about her and gently leads her away from the leering gaze of the mocking mob. It's a mob who obviously failed to understand how such a thing could be.

We don't always understand love. It's when we see it in action that we begin to know what love really is.

"You are to live with me many days; you must not be a prostitute or be intimate with any man, and I will live with you" (Hos. 3:3). So said Hosea, softly. And so Gomer is reinstated as the prophet's wife. Can you imagine what kind of a reception she was given by her three kids as they watched the two of them return home?!

It's a parable in which God expressed His everlasting love to Israel through the broken and humbled Hosea. Perhaps it was the first time that a prophet could really express what God feels toward His falling and fallen creations. In this, a most human story, we have witnessed the message of God's divine love for all of us for all times!

The Bible puts it so clearly, "For God so loved the world that he gave his one and only Son, that whoever believes in him shall not perish but have eternal life" (John 3:16).

TODAY'S BIBLE READING: Hosea 1:1-3:5

14.
THE MOTHER AND THE FAVORITE CHILD

Every mother has a favorite child! Really?! She just can't help it! After all, she is only a human mother. Yes . . . I have mine. This is the child for whom I shall feel a very special, motherly closeness. It is to this child that a love is offered that nobody else could possibly understand at the time or later.

My favorite child was born with a cleft lip and couldn't properly take milk from a bottle without filling his little tummy with air. He had colic all the time. He always seemed to be the one to need stitches in his head.

My favorite child is the son who broke his arm while climbing a tree on the very first day of his summer vacation! Who was sick with the mumps during Christmas! Who was so sick at her 13th birthday party she couldn't eat any of her favorite chocolate cake and had to watch all her invited friends gorge themselves.

My favorite child was the one whom was passed over and chosen last for school games. Who never quite made the grades that an older sibling had achieved. Who happened to be see the family pet struck by a car on the highway.

My favorite child had to wear a protective helmet to bed to protect the head injury from further injury. Who had a teacher who made life miserable for him in the fourth grade. Who I held in my arms all the way to the emergency room so stitches could be set. Who struggled with asthma.

My favorite child spent Christmas Eve away from the family for the first time because he forget to put gas into the tank and was stranded alone between college and home. Who on the first date couldn't get the car started in the fast-food parking lot where he'd taken her to eat following the ball game. Who had his first bicycle stolen.

My favorite child is the one who forgot all those carefully learned lines for the church school special Easter program. Who lost the money so lovingly earned and saved in order to buy one radio-controlled model plane. Who really messed up at the piano recital in front of all those people.

My favorite child, at her big moment as a cheerleader, fell flat on her face! Who was cut from the baseball team. Who dropped the winning touchdown pass in the end-zone. Who failed the most important rite of passage, a driver's license exam.

My favorite child is the one whom I disciplined for cheating. Whom I also grounded in front of a friend who happened to be visiting. Whom I told had been a royal mess-up in the family. Whom I over-reacted to.

My favorite child slammed doors in frustrated anger because of the way she had been treated by her "best" friend. Who cried when she was ignored by the "in" people in her high school. Who withdrew and refused to talk about it.

My favorite child always looked unkempt no matter what he put on. Who had a big date with the most wonderful girl in the world and his car was out of gas and had a flat tire on Saturday night.

My favorite child struggled with a bad temper that blew at the most inopportune times. He also couldn't decide on what he wanted to do with his life. Who was the 96th man when 95 had been chosen for med school. Who was jilted by the love of his life.

My favorite child was fired from a first "real" job because of a false accusation by another employee. My favorite child had to get married on a day that rained cats and dogs, miserable.

ALL MOTHERS EVERYWHERE HAVE THEIR FAVORITE CHILD! And it seems to always be the same one! THE ONE WHO NEEDS YOU AT THE MOMENT!

The one who needs you at the moment may be frustrated, hurt, happy, depressed, injured, rejected, self-centered, immature, selfish, disappointed, lonely, questioning, hungry, wondering, helpless, in love, misguided, or what-have-you.

This child may need you to hold on to . . . to scream at . . . to verbally attack . . . to hug . . . to dump on . . . to cry with . . . to encourage . . . to love . . . to vent . . . to use your credit card . . . to question and to always reverse the charges to.

But, perhaps, more than anything else . . . my favorite child simply needs a mother just to be there!

 TODAY'S BIBLE READING:
    1 Corinthians 13:1-13

15
GET ME TO THE
CHURCH ON TIME

Did you hear about the lady who had married four different husbands? She had outlived them all. However, in the order in which they were married, the first was a banker, next an actor, the third was a minister and the fourth was an undertaker. One for the money; two for the show; three to get ready; and four to go.

Yes, I know, that's pretty bad. Have you considered that when someone gets married, they say, "He gave away the bride." What they didn't tell you is that it may have cost him $8,000 to do it.

Most mothers enjoy weddings, or so I've observed. Let's talk a bit about an ancient wedding which took place, and five of the attendants didn't get to the church on time. If these five were like most young ladies, they must have dreamed and planned and prepared and dressed up for this big event. However, at the very last moment, it slipped through their grasp. This is a story filled with pathos and contrasts.

The setting is that Jesus Christ is now on the homestretch of His earthly ministry. With His death staring Him in the face . . . He tells this charming story about an Oriental wedding which had both a happy and sad ending. Jesus had this wonderful way of sharing truth, we call it a parable. A story with more than one meaning, some of which were hidden. This particular parable could fit into a class of "Parables about Wisdom and Folly." The Master storyteller captures our attention with a riveting line, "At that time the kingdom of heaven will be like ten virgins. . . ." Now don't try to find too much meaning in the significance of the oil, the sleeping, the vessels, and the lamps. This is the background which leads up to one question: Will you be ready when Jesus Christ comes for His Bride?

The background against which this story is told is important for our understanding. Jewish law called for the wedding to usually begin on a Wednesday, usually in the home of the bride's father or perhaps his brother, and uncle. That evening or almost any time after the ceremony begins, the bride and her bridesmaids would be on the lookout for the groom and his attendants. It was almost a game to guess when the groom would appear.

Another interpretation has it that as part of a typical Oriental wedding, a dowry would be negotiated. You must keep in mind that there was no courting as we do today, fathers did the planning and bargaining. When everything was settled the groom was finally free to claim his bride.

Pageantry and drama were part of this style of wedding. Sooner or later the haggling was resolved and the groom came, the time was unknown. He came to take the bride and her attendants back to his parental home where the wedding continued, sometimes as long as a week in celebration. If the delay would be too long, people became tired. The account says, "they all became drowsy and all fell asleep." Not that unusual.

The story is a message to Christians. These were not five virgins and five prostitutes. All were virgins, all had been invited to the wedding party, all had lamps, all had some oil to start with, all were sleeping, all were together with the bride, all had responded to the occasion, all were dressed alike . . . but five were wise and five were foolish.

At midnight the cry rang out, "Here's the bridegroom!" What a moment! There was a delay about his coming and there was darkness at his coming.

How important is the fact of a second coming of Jesus, the Heavenly Groom? Consider that there are 1,845 references to the Second Coming in 17 different Old Testament books. Out of the 260 chapters in the New Testament, there are 318 references to the Second Coming. This is about one out of every 30 verses. And 23 of the 27 New Testament books refer to the coming event. Also you need to put into perspective the importance in noting that in the Bible, for every written prophesy on His first coming, there are eight on the second coming. It is an important future event.

Outwardly these ten virgins looked alike, a very typical wedding party for the bride. The difference was in their supply of oil. The supply or lack of it made the difference. There's some debate, theologically, as to what the oil stands for. The majority of these theologians come down on the side of using oil as a symbol of the Holy Spirit or that having a full supply of oil represents the true believers. All ten had *some* oil. This division cuts deeply, half missed out. Would the half that missed be called "hypocrites"?

Can you imagine the panic and tears. Pounding on the door, yelling, screaming, throwing rocks at the door, kicking at it, throwing tantrums . . . nothing opened the door! There they stood, outside, listening to the sounds of the wedding going on inside. So near and yet so far. These were not bad girls, simply unprepared girls. They may have gotten by in a previous wedding party, but this one they missed. . . .

As you read this parable once more, there are some principles for living that come to mind:

1) THE PERSONAL EXPERIENCE OF BRING BORN AGAIN IS NOT TRANSFERABLE TO ANYBODY ELSE. God has no grandchildren! It's not an experience of mother or father or anybody else that gets any of us ready for heaven. It's a one-on-one, personal experience. We all come the same way, "by grace are we saved through faith, it is the gift of God."

2) LOST OPPORTUNITIES CANNOT BE RECOVERED! The five who ran out of oil went to buy some more, made their preparations, too late, the bridegroom and the rest of the wedding party were already out of sight and when caught up with, the door was already locked. Their time to prepare was past. The Bible is explicit, "Today is the day of salvation."

3) THE SECOND COMING WILL COME WITHOUT WARNING! He will come as a "thief in the night." He will "come in such an hour as you think not." He will come "as lightning from the east." This parable is not addressed to those who have never made any preparation, but to those who have not made sufficient preparation. What a tragedy to have lived a life of pretend Christianity, to dress like a Christian, to act like a Christian, when you could have been honest and had all the fun of human living. But to have gone through all the motions and actions for years and miss the ultimate event of what being a Christian is all about . . . nothing could be as frightening as this! So near, yet so far . . . almost — just about — missing by the skin of your teeth. But the real problem is that it is so easy to pretend, too easy to pretend.

TODAY'S BIBLE READING:
      Matthew 25:1-46

16.
OUT OF
THE NEST

It's a springtime ritual which is repeated millions of times every year. The mother bird gives her timid, frightened youngster that gentle but firm nudge which sends the baby robin sailing into nothingness from the security of the nest. You hold your breath . . . the young bird wobbles and kind of flops through space . . . you are sure that it will sail right into the ground or any number of obstacles nearby. But at the very last moment, the small, inexperienced wings are spread enough to lift the little bird into the safety of the branch of a nearby tree. The mother lights on the same limb, chattering encouragement . . . getting the little one ready for the next life experience.

This past spring, it was my privilege to share and listen as a lonely couple talked about the vast emptiness that had invaded their lives since their only child had moved away to a distant city to work on an advanced degree at a university. And then . . . I thought about some of the differences between robins and people, particularly mother robins and people. Will that mother bird be able to identify her offspring a year or two years from the nudge out of the nest? It doesn't seem so, does it? Birds don't have the same kind of long-term, continuing family relationships as human beings.

The mother bird's responsibility seems to be to teach her little ones to be able to fly as quickly as possible. There are dangers should the little bird remain nest-bound too long. Predators will prey on birds which never leave the nest.

But with people we see that the opposite can be true. Mothers, in the scheme of things, are supposed to train, nurture, and prepare their children to cope with adulthood which will eventually be their challenge. But mothers, being mothers, sometimes find it so hard to turn them loose, let alone nudge them out of the nest. The human tendency is to hold on, shield our kids from the tough realities of an unfair world as long as possible.

As a clergyman, it's my privilege to observe life from a different perspective. We, the best man, groomsmen, pastor, along with the bride's father, were patiently waiting for the ceremony to begin. The groom was not present for some reason, but the father of the bride was absolutely beside himself, pacing back and forth and mumbling under his breath. Finally, I asked him what was the problem and perhaps he'd like to sit down and relax.

He turned to me and said, "What man in his right mind wants to give away his baby girl?" I sympathized but it wasn't enough. He went on, "Besides, it's like giving a rare and beautiful Stradivarious violin to a gorilla!" Wow!

Well, the wedding came off without a hitch, except for a now lonely father. Oh, yes, this story has a happy ending. Later, his daughter gave birth to a baby boy. One look at the happy grandfather said it all . . . the son-in-law, that gorilla, was okay because there was now the most wonderful grandchild ever born! It's tough to let go.

What do you suppose goes through the bird-brain of a robin as she nudges her baby out of the nest? Does she have feelings? Does she understand the process? Or is she simply doing by instinct the responsibilities granted her by the Creator? Is she just following the born-in directions she has been given? Do you think there just might have been even a slight reluctance in that nudge she gave her baby? Was she capable of expressing any kind of maternal instinct? Did she have any misgivings as she watched those small wings attempt a first flight?

May God bless you . . . all of you lonely mothers, everywhere. And also may God bless all of the mother birds for the beauty you have created, all the songs you sing, all the sacrifices you have made to sit on a nest, all the meals you have given up to feed the babies, and the life lessons you have given! My hope is simply this . . . that all human mothers have trained the little ones as well. It's a rough, tough, unsympathetic, difficult world out there. When the final nudge has been given . . . it's too late. The task must have been begun long before the nudge.

And . . . Mother, I am sure that you will shed a tear or two, or have already done so. You will likely hesitate when your time comes to give that final nudge. But because you are a mother, you will give it, you will do it, you must. And . . . this is called: THE NUDGE OF LOVE!

TODAY'S BIBLE READING:
Matthew 6:25–7:12

17.
THE MOST ESSENTIAL CHARACTER TRAIT

The character trait I nominate as being most essential is: UNCONDITIONAL LOVE! A sacrificial love, the kind of love that God shows towards all of us alike. It's produced in our hearts by a God who is love. This love is a deliberate desire for the highest good of the object of love, and is manifested in sacrificial actions for that person's good. The world will never believe that God is love until others can see this kind of love in all kinds of human experiences.

Little Chad was a quiet, shy kid. One day he came home and told his mother he'd like to make a "valentine" for everyone in his class. Her heart sank. She thought, *I wish he wouldn't do that*. She had watched the other children when they walked home from school. Her Chad was always alone and walked behind the others. Chad was never included. But he insisted, so she purchased paper, glue, and crayons. Then for weeks, night after night, Chad painstakingly made 35 valentines, his expressions of love.

Valentine's Day dawned and Chad was beside himself with excitement. He carefully stacked them up, bagged them, and bolted out the door. His mother decided to bake his favorite cookies and serve them nice and warm with a cool glass of milk, his "bestest" snack, when he came home from school. She just knew he would be disappointed and maybe that would ease the pain. It hurt to think that he would not get many valentines, maybe none at all.

That afternoon, cookies and milk ready, she heard the kids outside. She looked out the window and sure enough, the kids were laughing and having a good time. But as always, there was Chad in the rear. He walked faster than usual. She fully expected him to burst into tears as soon as he got inside. His hands were empty, she noticed, and when the door opened she choked back her tears.

"I baked your favorite cookies and here's a glass of milk," she said. But he hardly heard her words . . . he just marched right on by, his face aglow. . . . And all he could say was "Not a one! Not a one! Not a single one!"

And then he added, "I didn't forget a one, not a single one!"

When you first became a Christian . . . the Spirit of God entered your life and confirmed that a new relationship had been established. "The Spirit himself testifies with our spirit that we are God's children" (Rom. 8:16).

God's Spirit within us produces LOVE, God's kind of love, sacrificial love! And as long as we are dependent upon God for our strength and are obedient to the written Word, we experience the grace of a new Christian's "first love." But, therein also lies a problem. It is possible to lose that first love. It is possible to grieve the Spirit of God and leave that first love. This is clearly stated in Revelation 2:1-5 and along with the solution to renew it if it has been lost.

In simple language, we can lose our first love when we lose our daily awareness of our need for God. Our need brought us to God, but once God has begun to meet our needs, there is a tendency to forget that we have them.

Here's a checklist, some evidences that we may have left our "first love" for God, and for His people:

WHEN I cease to treat every other person as I would the Lord, then I have left my first love (Matt. 25:40; John 13:34).

WHEN I begin to view the commands of Jesus Christ as restrictions to my happiness rather than expressions of His love, I have left my first love (John 14:21).

WHEN I inwardly strive for the acclaim which this world can give me rather than the approval of the Lord, I have left it (1 John 2:15).

WHEN I fail to make Jesus Christ or His words known to others because I fear rejection, I have left my first love (John 15:20).

WHEN I refuse to give up an activity which I know is offending any weaker persons or causing them to stumble, I have left my first love (Rom. 14:15).

WHEN I have become complacent and uncaring about the worldly conditions and sin around me, I have left it (Matt. 24:12).

WHEN I no longer am able to forgive another person who may have offended me, I have left my first love (1 John 4:20).

Mother Teresa of Calcutta said: "Spread love everywhere you go: first of all in your own house. Give love to your children, to your spouse, to a next door neighbor. Let no one ever come to you without leaving better and happier. Be the living expression of God's kindness; kindness in your face, kindness in your eyes, kindness in your smile, kindness in your warm greeting."

If your first love is waning, or almost gone, the key to restoration is found in Revelation 2:5, "Remember the height from which you have fallen. Repent and do the things you did at first!"

Simply . . . REMEMBER . . . REPENT . . . and DO! Remember . . . what was it like at the very first, recall that characteristic of love and how it was manifested in and through your life. Repent — to repent is do an about face, to be sorry for the current condition and turn around and head back in the right direction. Do — actions testify of what takes place on the inside. Do what you know is a right action.

Love is the key to the universe which unlocks all doors! For this very reason we are to make every effort to add to our lifestyle, love!

TODAY'S BIBLE READING: John 3:1-36

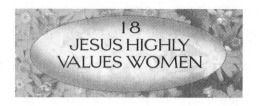

18
JESUS HIGHLY VALUES WOMEN

Read with me what some famous mothers could have said to their better-known sons:

Alexander's the Great's mother: "How many times do I have to tell you . . . you can't have everything!"

Franz Schubert's mother: "Take my advice, son. Never start anything you can't finish!"

Achilles' mother: "Stop imagining things. There's nothing wrong with your heel!"

Do you realize the obvious? Women make up more than half the population of this world! But . . . too often their, your contributions have been downplayed! The fact is that society and the home and the church desperately need the influence of women! Why? Women are primarily the ones who pass on our culture and shape our values. Women especially shape the youth and children of our nation! WOMEN EXERT A PROFOUND INFLUENCE!

Women are co-creators with the God of this universe. Women are able to conceive and bear new life. Talk about something that is awesome! But the role of mother and homemaker have fallen into disrepute and serious neglect.

Dee Jepson, wife of the former Senator from Iowa writes: "I can recall a time in Washington, DC, when I spoke in a discussion before a national committee of a large denominational church. In the course of my discussion I mentioned the word 'family' and drew audible groans from the audience. I wanted to weep, not because those present disagreed with me, that wasn't the point, but it grieved me that the family, which is God's idea and which is the basic unit of government within a nation, could be viewed with disdain even in the church."

Here's where it all began: Then God said, "Let us make man in our image, in our likeness, and let THEM rule over the fish of the sea and the birds of the air, over the livestock, over all the earth, and over all the creatures that move along the ground." So God created man in his own image, in the image of God he created him;

male and FEMALE he created THEM (Gen. 1:26-27;NIV).

Now let's take another look at a truth that has been forgotten by society and by the church, too often . . . JESUS CHRIST HIGHLY VALUED WOMEN!

This, perhaps, is one of the best-kept, untold secrets about Christianity! Jesus values women! The church has not done a very good job at letting women or society know this truth. You need to know this as truth, not because of your own personal merits but because of the qualities that God has given you to use on and for His behalf.

Ladies, women, mothers . . . you have a high and wonderful calling! You have a great challenge. The world needs to hear that JESUS CHRIST VALUES WOMEN!

Jesus is the liberator, the one who frees women from sin and bondage . . . as well as from the circumstances and distortions of our culture. God today is calling on women to play an important role in His eternal plan. Something very vital and necessary to the quality of life will be lost if women to not respond to this call. For too long and too often, the Church has taught and women have accepted the concept that the Bible somehow relegates them to being second class citizens in the plan of God! Not true! Not!

CONSIDER: God chose Mary to give birth to His Son when He was sent to this world. The eternal Son of God entered into this world just like all of us . . . through the womb of a woman! It didn't have to be that way . . . Jesus could have come out of the desert, fully matured, to begin His ministry.

Instead, God chose a woman, an unlikely one at that. Mary was likely poor, quite young, and not yet married. She came from the most insignificant of all villages. People laughed when they talked about Nazareth and asked, "Can any good thing come out of Nazareth?"

But Mary must have been chosen based on some very significant and important character traits . . . humility and a determination to do the will of God no matter what the cost. "I am the Lord's servant," Mary answered. "May it be to me as you have said" (Luke 1:38). This is the kind of dedication and humility needed by all of us.

CONSIDER: Jesus told the Samaritan woman at the well the greatest life secret in the world. What secret? That He, Jesus, was the long-awaited Messiah and that He was the answer to entering eternal life! This woman was another most unlikely choice. The Jews hated the Samaritans. The typical rabbi refused to talk to any woman in public. But even more than this, this Samaritan woman had a terrible reputation as a home-wrecker in her home town. He told her about living water and she believed Him. She acted on her belief and this is another thing that women are very good at doing.

CONSIDER: Think about two sisters, Mary and Martha. You know the details. But there is one point often over-looked in this story. In the society of Jesus' day, women were NOT to be taught by a rabbi or teacher. They were completely cut off from the current religious system.

Jesus cut across this cultural barrier to elevate women to a position of equality! He said that Mary had chosen the better part, to be with Him, to learn from Him.

CONSIDER: Who were the first people at the tomb? Women! To whom did Jesus make His first appearance when He rose from the grave? To a woman! Who was the first evangelist to tell the good news of His resurrection? A woman! She went into her town to tell the others, most notably the hidden disciples, that He was alive!

Let's conclude that the Bible does not present women as second-class citizens in the kingdom of God! Let's acknowledge that women were and are very important and essential to God's plan in our today's world!

JESUS HIGHLY VALUES WOMEN!

TODAY'S BIBLE READING:
  Luke 1:26-56; Mark 16:1-11

19.
FIVE MATERNAL INSIGHTS

It all started with excitement! It began with an angel making an appearance to Mary to tell her that she would conceive of the Holy Spirit and become the earthly mother to the only Son of God! Well . . . it began much earlier, the first recorded promise of the coming Saviour was prophesied by the Lord God in Genesis 3:15, "And I will put enmity between you and the woman, and between your offspring and hers; he will crush your head and you will strike his heel."

From the moment the angel spoke, Jesus impacted people. Think of some of those people — an earthly, human father, Joseph; his mother, Mary; close friends such as Lazarus and his sisters Mary and Martha; a chosen band of 12, including one who would turn on Him, Judas; and a whole host of other earthly people were touched. In honor of these human relationships here are five maternal insights into the life of Christ:

THE CARPENTER'S MOTHER

I could only shake my head.
Midway through the engagement
something went wrong.
But that mule-headed man
would not listen to logic.
"The law says, Joseph, the law says.
The shame would kill her anyway.

Stoning will be merciful.
It happens all the time, Joseph.
Think of the family, Joseph, think of our name.
Put her out, Joseph.
You must at least put her out
Or you are no son of mine."
But he only shook his head.

MOTHER OF MAGDALA

I haven't seen her since
she was thirteen.
I hear about her now
and then. She's seen
among the men they say
who follow Him,
the Nazarene.

But then that's why she left
she's always been
a girl who's far too much
among men.
And I am left alone
while she goes about
among the men.

LAZARUS' MOTHER

I never lost as much but twice,*
My husband, then my son;
But wailing for my son was hushed
Before the week was done.

The Teacher called my Lazarus
Out of the grave back then.
And though he's wrapped in death once more,
I know he'll live again.

*From Emily Dickinson

JUDAS' MOTHER

He never was a happy soul.
He never could enjoy
A game, or just let loose
Like any other boy.

He wore a cloud in infancy
Or so it seemed to me;
The coos and clucks I paid to him
Did nothing I could see.

Then as his limbs would lengthen out,
His face would do the same.
He wore a melancholy look
The way he wore his name.

But when the Teacher took him on,
I thought great things would come,
That following that Teacher might
Improve his manner some.

My hopeful heart was broken, though; Such things were not to be.
The Teacher did no good at all; For my poor son and me.

PETER'S MOTHER-IN-LAW

He changes hot to health, delirium to sense;
He raised me from a bed ablaze with virulence.
He changes naught to is, and weakness into strength;
He sparked my shortened days alive with fervid length.[10]

TODAY'S BIBLE READING: John 1:1-51

20.
MOTHER-IN-LAW!

We've all been bombarded by the mother-in-law jokes and stories. Let me set the record straight for all times . . . my mother-in-law was a wonderful lady whom I loved and adored. Well, now that that has been set straight — did you hear about the disgruntled fellow who claims that the reason Adam lived in paradise was that he had no mother-in-law? Then, there was the pastor who announced from the pulpit that a certain member of the congregation "has had the loud-speaker system installed in our church in loving memory of his mother-in-law." Enough, yet!

In the Bible, from the Book of Ruth, there is an exquisite bit of literature. It follows immediately after the blood-stained stories of the Book of Judges. I hope you have read this story lately because it's the background for this meditation.

The story is simple . . . the rains had failed to fall in Bethlehem country and the consequent harvests were small. A certain family composed of husband, wife, and two boys find it tough to keep the wolf away from the door. Elimelech, the husband, can find no work, and Naomi, wife and mother, goes through the daily torture of being asked for food she can't supply.

Over a family confab they decide to go the land of Moab because of being driven by hunger. Moab wasn't far off physically, but spiritually and morally, a great ways off. But in this new land they seem to have been welcomed among these strangers. Their children grew up playing with heathen playmates . . . eventually, these two Jewish boys fell in love with two Moabite girls. A calamity for a Jewish family . . . but they seemed to make the best of it. They married and Naomi and Elimelech supported this decision.

Then . . . disaster came into this family — Elimelech died. Husband and father gone! Now Naomi was left with the family responsibilities. Her daughters-in-law had seen her in joy, now they saw her in sorrow.

Disaster strikes again . . . both boys died! Naomi is not only a widow, now she is without children. There is now no reason to stay in this strange land so she decides to return back home. Here two daughters-in-law were to go with her as far as the border of Moab, there to bid a final farewell. These three sad women make their journey. At the border, Orpah tells Naomi goodbye, parts with real grief and regret, for she has learned to love her mother-in-law with a genuine love. If we listen carefully, we can still hear some of those sobs of parting.

Then . . . it's Ruth's time to say goodbye. We watch a sacred moment as she flings her arms about Naomi's neck and there she clings. Naomi encourages her to leave and go back with her sister-in-law. But Ruth only clings harder. Here she makes a confession of love. Nothing finer has ever been written in all of human literature. It was made from a daughter-in-law to a mother-in-law! It's the confession of youth to age . . . springtime holding to winter . . . June flinging its arms in a passionate tenderness around the neck of November.

Ruth replied, "Don't urge me to leave you or to turn back from you. Where you go I will go, and where you stay I will stay. Your people will be my people and your God my God. Where you die I will die, and there I will be buried. May the Lord deal with me, be it ever so severely, if anything but death separates you and me" (Ruth 1:16-18).

And the people of the little village of Bethlehem had something interesting to talk about a few days later. Two strange women had come their way, women who were poverty-stricken and homeless. One a Jew, the other a Gentile! Neither of them would have been particularly welcomed. Naomi had left her place in this community . . . Ruth, the Moabite had never had any place.

The days that followed were a bit sad and bitter, but the younger woman, with courage, refuses to be a burden. Instead she will be the support of the mother of her dead husband. She takes upon herself the menial task of being a gleaner. It's harvest time and she goes out into the fields to glean, to pick up the grain that is missed by the harvesters. It was as humble a work as could be done in Israel at that time. It was that or starve.

Now . . . the story takes an interesting turn. It happens that in the providence of God the field in which she gleans belongs to the very rich and prosperous Boaz! His attention is drawn to the winsome, beautiful, vivacious, young woman from Moab. She happens to be one of those young ladies with a superior beauty born out of superior character. Well, one thing leads to another. And, of course, Naomi is very interested in what is happening. Perhaps, by instinct, she is a matchmaker. So she sets about the delicate task of helping them to understand each other. Because of her wise advice things turn out just as they ought to turn out and as the saying goes, "they lived happily ever after!"

Who is the heroine of this exquisite story? I believe it is Naomi, the mother-in-law! And please read or re-read the story of Ruth. But one more thing . . . were we privileged to sit down beside Naomi in her Father's house, today, she could teach us some wonderful lessons on living. I can only surmise . . . but I think these would be at least two of them:

1) LIFE'S GREATEST LOSSES, THROUGH THE GRACE OF GOD, CAN BECOME ITS RICHEST GAINS! She could tell you of the black despair of those days when driven from her home by the cruel hand of poverty. She could talk about the aching pain over losses of loved ones. This woman had learned the fine art of capitalizing on her calamities. In the midst of poverty and tragedy and loss she kept firm her faith in her God. She found that His grace was sufficient for all her days.

So mother, whoever, and wherever you might be today in life's journey, hold on to your faith! Don't give up! Joy will return one of these days!

2) THERE IS POWER TO BLESS OTHERS IN A CONSECRATED LIFE! Naomi was a very hidden and obscure person. Had you walked by her side as, hunger driven, she left her native land, she likely would not have told you anything of the great destiny that was ahead for her! She never dreamed of enriching the world as she did! It never occurred to her that she was to be one of the great light-bringers of all the centuries. This world could not have gotten along without Naomi! It could not for the simple reason that Naomi led Ruth into a personal knowledge and relationship with God and into the fellowship of His people.

How did Ruth come to make such a confession: "Your people will be my people . . . and your God will be my God"? Because of her mother-in-law! She fell in love with a wonderful lady and then fell in love with that lady's God. Naomi made possible Ruth's second successful marriage!

Then one day . . . a baby was born into this new home of Ruth and Boaz. The years went by and there was another baby born among those Judean hills with sunshine tangled in his hair and countless songs pent up in his heart. So he sang and battled and sinned and repented and everybody loved him as one of the greatest leaders this world has ever seen. We still thank God for David! And did you know that King David was Ruth's grandbaby?!

More years went by and there was another burst of special heavenly light on those same Judean hills, there was music from a country where everybody sings! It was an angelic choir announcing for all the world to hear, especially those shepherds, about a Saviour . . . who is Christ the Lord! And this was another of Ruth's grandbabies!

But in the grand and glorious purpose of God, neither David nor David's greater Son would have been possible without Naomi . . . mother-in-law! So one woman, remaining true to God no matter how difficult life had become, became the roadway along which the Almighty walked to the accomplishment of His great purpose . . . to bring the Saviour into the world!

I say, hats off to all godly mothers-in-law! Bless you, ma'am!

TODAY'S BIBLE READING: Ruth 1:1-22; 4:13-22

21.
THE LOST DOG

Every Sunday afternoon, this particular family went for a drive out in the country after their lunch and a quick nap. It was a tradition that seemed to work quite well until the kids became teens . . . oh, well, that's another story. On one such country drive they were about six miles onto a gravel road. There was nothing for miles around except for a small hill with a little dirt road ascending to the top of the hill from the gravel road. As they passed by the desolate dirt road, they passed a dog that barked and seemed to be lost. But the dog seemed friendly. The kids immediately set up a howl, "Can we take him home?" "We can't just leave him alone way out here!" "Please, mom!" "Mmomm, pleeaassse!"

So the mother, being a pushover for lost and strayed dogs and cats, discussed their options. The kids prevailed, Dad caved, and Mom agreed that they just could not leave a lost dog alone. So they backed up the car to the dirt road and compassionately allowed the dog into the car. The dog willingly hopped into the back seat and curled up on the kids' laps. Immediately the family fell in love with their new friend. The dog seemed happy with the arrangement as he contentedly wagged his tail. It was one of those love at first sight kind of happenings.

After a couple of days, the mother suggested at the dinner table that they had better make sure someone was not looking for this lost dog. So they put a small ad in the local weekly paper. The first day the ad was printed, a man called about the dog. He identified the dog over the phone, found out the address, and said he would come by to get it.

When the farmer arrived, he and his dog had a joyous reunion. He paid the family a reward for the dog . . . plus their expenses incurred for the newspaper ad. The family was so attached to the dog by this time that they followed the man and his dog to his pickup that was parked in their driveway. The man opened the door and the dog hopped into the passenger seat. He sat up like he belonged there.

Than the man turned to the family before getting into the truck and said, "I sure am sorry about the trouble my dog caused you. I've never had a bit of trouble with him before. He usually stays close to the house. And I live about six and a half miles from the highway on a dirt road a half a mile from the gravel road. He's never strayed much past the gravel road as far as I know." A case of mistaken identity hits once more!

It's so easy to do . . . mistaking something or other for the real thing. Sometimes it's just an honest mistake.

When Jesus was 12 years old, His mother and father made the same kind of mistake. They assumed He was in their traveling company when He was not. "Thinking He was in their company, they traveled on for a day . . . then they began looking for Him" This assumption cost them a day's travel back to Jerusalem, plus two spent in the search to find Him. On the third day they came across him in the temple sitting among the teachers and asking them questions.

It's easy to assume that your kids are with you, not on drugs, and know all they should know about dating and sexuality. We assume that they are better equipped to face life than they may be. But have you checked lately?

The tendency in life is to take things easy. The most tragic of assumptions would be to assume that Jesus is traveling through life with you . . . only to realize one day that He has been left behind in the crush of life activities.

Many of us are like the lady who read that dogs were healthier if fed a teaspoon of cod liver oil each day. So every day she followed the same routine . . . she chased her dog until she caught it, wrestled it down, and managed to force the fishy remedy down the poor dog's throat. One day, in the middle of this grueling contest of wills and medical efforts . . . the bottle was kicked over! With a sigh she loosened her grip on the dog so she could wipe up the spreading mess on her kitchen floor. To her surprise, the dog trotted over to the puddle and began lapping up what had been spilled. THE DOG LOVED COD LIVER OIL! It was just the method of application to which the dog objected.

Perhaps we, too, need to re-evaluate some of our methods and assumptions! With God's help, this is also a real possibility. Try it . . . you may find lots of surprises awaiting you!

TODAY'S BIBLE READING: Luke 2:21-52

22.
THE FACE OF GOD

Following the devastating earthquake that struck Ecuador in 1988, an Indianapolis newspaper sent John Jackson, a photographer, to cover the story for their readers. One thing touched him more than anything else . . . the human suffering which he saw everywhere. He wrote a poem which was published in the October 10, 1988, issue of *Monday Morning*. Here it is:

THE FACE OF GOD

The line was long
But moving briskly
And in that line
At the very end
Stood a young girl
About twelve years of age.
She waited patiently as those
At the front of that long line
Received a little rice,
Some canned goods,
Or a little fruit.
Slowly but surely
She was getting closer

To the front of that line,
Closer to the food.
From time to time
She would glance
Across the street.
She did not notice
The growing concern
On the faces of those
Distributing the food.
The food was running out.
Their anxiety began to show,
But she did not notice.
Her attention seemed always

To focus on three figures
Under the trees across the street.
At long last she stepped forward
To get her food
But the only thing left
Was the lonely banana.
The workers were almost
Ashamed to tell her
That was all that was left.
She did not seem to mind
To get that solitary banana.
Quietly she took the precious gift
And ran across the street
Where three small children
Waited. Perhaps her sisters

And a brother.
Very deliberately
She peeled the banana
And very carefully
Divided the banana
Into three equal parts,
Placing the precious food
In the eager hands
Of those three younger ones.
One for you, one for you.
She then sat down
And licked the inside
Of that banana peel.
In that moment I swear
I SAW THE FACE OF GOD![11]

TODAY'S BIBLE READING: Matthew 25:14-46

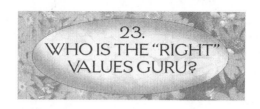

23.
WHO IS THE "RIGHT" VALUES GURU?

Much is being made about what are the "right" values which should be taught to our kids. Brenda Turner, senior associate editor, wrote an article for *USA Weekend*. She pointed out that five people have emerged in the national focus on family values. Let's take a look at these five which Turner has identified:

1) Dan Quayle, the vice president who served with President George Bush. His major contention is that the traditional two-parent families still work the best. They have been the best plan and will always be the best plan for American families. His book, which is composed of interviews of a number of American families, is entitled: *The American Family*.

2) Hillary Clinton, Democratic first lady in the Clinton White House. She is more than a first lady, she is also a leading children's activist. She wrote, *It Takes a Village: and Other Lessons Children Teach Us*. Her major premise is that it takes the government, churches, the business community, and the media to help parents most effectively raise their kids. According to her, government plays a very crucial role in seeing to it that this happens.

3) William Bennett, who has written the following three books: *The Book of Virtues, The Children's Book of Virtues*, and *The Moral Compass*. Mr. Bennett is the former secretary of education. Bennett's major thrust is that he feels virtues and values are important and need to be restored to the nation's consciousness and in turn to be lived out by the children. He argues that morality should be taught and can be taught by teaching to our children some of the classic stories of virtue.

4) Jonathan Kozol, author of *Amazing Grace: the Lives of Children and the Conscience of a Nation*, is a journalist and Harvard graduate who uses the statistic that 23 percent of all American children live at or

beneath the line of poverty, and that poverty is the main cause of the current family disintegration. Then he pleads that there must be a greater awareness by the "haves," mainly the middle and upper classes, for the very acute needs presented by the poor children in our nation.

5) Mary Pipher has written *Reviving Ophelia* and *The Shelter of Each Other*. Mary works as a clinical psychologist and lives in Nebraska. She tells us that the lower "junk values" of our American culture is what is waging the war against the family. She maintains that the family must fight back against the forces of media, pop psychology, and addictive technologies. Pipher further claims that adults "are no longer teaching children to be human, and children are no longer learning how to be human from real people who care about them."

The writer Brenda Turner also included some very frightening statistics in her *Weekend* article:

- Parents in the nineties spend 40 percent less time with their kids than in the 1950s!
- In the 1990s, twice as many kids (18.5 million) live in single parent homes as in the 1970s!
- Today, the average daily time parents spend with the other is about 20 minutes!
- By the time children enter junior high they have seen 8,000 TV murders take place!
- One-eighth of all parents abuse alcohol!
- One-third of all teenagers have had sex by eighth grade!

Now comes the big question: MOTHER . . . WHO do you want to teach basic values to your children? Which of the five above would you trust with your child's value system? Which philosophy of values are you ready to embrace? Or . . . will it be done by default? Do you think that somehow it just will happen?

The very bottom line is that YOU are the person who should be teaching values, you should be the value guru in the life of your child! That has been one of the God-given responsibilities for mothers, as well as fathers, from the time the family was first established! God not only holds you responsible for this duty . . . He also gives explicit ways in which this must be done.

"These commandments that I give you today are to be upon your hearts" (Deut. 6:6). It starts with Mom and Dad who have embraced a godly value system. The very centerpiece of values tells us to "Love the Lord your God with all your heart and with all your soul and with all your strength" (Mark 12:30).

Here is where it begins! God at the center, and everything radiates out from this hub. When this principle is first established with YOU, then you can pass it along to kids.

"Impress them on your children, talk about them when you sit at home and when you walk along the road, when you lie down and when you get up" (Deut. 6:7). There is a constant about this wonderful task. You don't do it once and then forget it. Repetition is the key! At home, when you travel, when it's time for bed, and when little heads get up in the morning. Not only talk about them, impress them. There is an urgency because here are foundational principles for life! Mom and Dad have the primary responsibility of putting values into the fabric of their kids.

"Tie them as symbols on your hands and bind them on your foreheads" (Deut. 6:8). Then the hands and the head are always a reminder of the importance of these commandments. A child without a value system is like a ship without an anchor. What will be there when the storms of life blow down on that child? Principles which apply to all of life will hold that child safe and secure. Do it while they are young so they can guide an entire lifetime.

"Write them on the doorframes of your houses and on your gates" (Deut. 6:9). The home is the place where values are to be learned . . . on the doorframes. Every time a child enters or exits, let them be reminded of these values. On the gates is a reminder that the values are to be carried to the outside world, too. It's a notice to all who pass by that here is a diligent home intent upon working the values into all of life for children. While children are still impressionable, before they have been exposed to another's values or to no values at all, get the jump early! Be diligent! Be exacting!

So, who do you want to set and teach values to your kids? Mom . . . this is the moment to step up to the challenge and say, "I AM THE ONE TO TEACH LIFE VALUES TO MY CHILDREN!" And further, "God being my helper, I will be consistent in building godly values line by line, precept upon precept, principle upon principle, until my child is ready to face life!"

 TODAY'S BIBLE READING:
Deuteronomy 28:1-48

24.
OVERCOMING ADVERSITY

Let me introduce you to a very special lady named Joni Dunn. She was an active, out-of-doors, athletic person. She was an intermediate skier who enjoyed the sport — not outstanding, just intermediate. While skiing on a Vermont mountain in 1972, she skidded off the trail, plunged about 100 feet into a deep ravine, fracturing her spine in seven places, as well as fracturing her neck and skull.

At first, doctors held little hope for Dunn's survival. "I heard them say, 'She won't make it through the night,'" Dunn remembers. "I knew if I stopped concentrating on living, I would die.

"I had always handled my problems along with everyone else's. Now I was as dependent as a baby. When they brought my three-year-old son Brian to the hospital, he reached out his arms. I wanted to touch him, but I couldn't move."

It would be nearly a year and a half before Joni was able to hug her son. Meanwhile, an operation to save her from total paralysis, and subsequently a body cast, took two inches off her height and left her hunch-backed. "My body seemed entirely alien to me," she recalls. "I used to stare at my back in the mirror and just cry."

Still dangerously weak but barely recovering, Joni began swimming therapy at the suggestion of her team of doctors. In 1975 she became a member of the local YMCA in Greenwich, Connecticut, along with her son, and managed to dog-paddle the length of the pool two or three times a week.

She continued with her story, "Just moving caused me incredible pain. But I knew I had to do this. I came from a very disciplined Dutch Reform family in Illinois. That discipline has always been with me and it makes me strong." Before long, Joni was able to swim half a mile in the pool without stopping for a rest.

Then she began to take little jogs around her neighborhood.

"The doctors told me not to over-exert myself, but after a year of running I began to feel normal again and stopped listening to them," says Dunn. She then began adding other types and kinds of exercises such as bicycle riding. These began to flatten the hump on her back.

Then it was as if she had blown a gasket or something. It was quite another story. The now 43-year-old Joni Dunn, who had never performed a single sit-up before the skiing accident, came up with the idea that she should enter the "Hawaiian Ironman Triathlon." This event is an incredible test of endurance and stamina and strength. This triathlon consisted of starting with 2.4 miles of swimming which was followed by 112 miles of tough bicycle riding, with the final event consisting of running the marathon, 26.3 miles!

Dunn said, "Everybody looked at me like I was a crazy lady. When I began training for the triathlon, I used to wake up in the middle of the night so scared . . . it was the same feeling as when I first started walking after the accident."

The training regimen continued and finally culminated in the 1985 Hawaiian Ironman Triathlon. How did she do? "At the start of the race I jumped in the water with all these world-class athletes . . . and for a moment felt paralyzed. I thought, *What am I doing here?* Then I realized I've never quit at anything in my life and I started to stroke."

Well . . . how did she really do? Joni Dunn defeated all the other women in her age category and she set a new record time in doing it![12]

Reading about such a feat gives a new appreciation for the human spirit! But did you pick up out of her narrative the real key? The secret which she capitalized on to make it happen? You can read her secret in the sixth paragraph of this story: DISCIPLINE! The discipline came out of her family and church upbringing.

The word "discipline" is almost lost in today's culture. Nobody wants to pay the price anymore. We live in this instant-everything kind of mindset culture. And if anything exacts too much by way of sacrifice, too much discipline, too much effort . . . there is a tendency to forget about it. But every now and then we find that special person who overcomes the natural inertia coming from living in our take-it-easy kind of world. Joni Dunn is a challenge to all of us who have decided to take it easy.

This word "discipline" has all kinds of shades of meaning. Consider that to be disciplined means: diligent exercise, practice, preparation, indoctrination, enforcement of rules, drilling, schooling, method, regulated activity, prescribed habit, regimen, self-enforced practice, to be trained, and to stick to the rules.

The basic root word for "discipline" and "disciple" are one and the same. To become a disciple is to be disciplined, disciplined by self as well as by the Word of God. Nothing of real value is ever accomplished without self-discipline. You can be disciplined by others . . . but until it becomes "self-discipline" it has no value. It's taking the policeman off the corner and placing it in your life.

There is a tremendous need for this character value to be in the life and lifestyle of every mother so that she may know how to instill it in the life and living of another, namely our own kids.

Self-discipline or self-control means that we are restraining ourselves. But from what? What is it that we are to keep ourselves from doing?

The Greek word for self-control is "egkrateia" and it is made up of two roots: "en" meaning to be infused with or by, and "kratos" which means vigor, dominion, power, or strength. Thus, to have "egkrateia" or self-control or self-discipline is to have a strong will, but one held firmly in check.

The bottom line is simply that we are to develop self-control so that we can be more like Jesus Christ, so that we may experience more of His power and presence in our lives, and so that it can be passed on to others. Self-discipline is a form of worship before God. It is a living out of His commands by doing what He commands us to do so that God can fully trust us. Other people learn to trust us as they observe this character quality being lived out in our lives.

Max Lucado wrote: "I am a spiritual being. After this body is dead, my spirit will soar. I refuse to let what will rot, rule the eternal. I choose self-control. I will be drunk only by joy. I will be impassioned only by my faith. I will be influenced only by God. I will be taught only by Christ. I choose self-control."

TODAY'S BIBLE READING: Daniel 1:1-20

25.
I DARE YOU TO SEARCH ME

Do you enjoy war stories . . . especially those with intrigue — real-life spy stories, with a real heroine? If this is not your choice in reading, you might enjoy this one, nevertheless. It originally appeared as a feature story in the July 19, 1948, edition of *Time* magazine under the heading of "National Affair," with the sub-heading, "Heroes . . . a Heroine."

The story featured a young lady called "Joey." She was really Mrs. Josefina Guerrero from the high society register of Manila in the Philippines. She was awarded the "Medal of Honor" for her work as a spy during World War II for our side. Why? Because of all the secret maps and messages she carried back and forth across enemy lines many times. She was never caught, never apprehended, never searched, and never discovered.

Josefina Guerrero had it all going her way . . . young, beautiful, with a wealthy husband who was a medical student at the Santo Tomas University. She was the toast of the society whirl. But that was before the war came. This all changed when the Japanese invaded the Philippines. Josefina, together with the other young matrons of Manila, began to help where they could. They provided food, clothing, and medicine to many of the prisoners of war.

Then the Americans landed on Leyte . . . it was then that Joey offered herself to the Americans as a spy and promising to be the very best spy they had ever had. She was already experienced because of some of her work with the Manilan underground. The American officers who interviewed her also agreed with her youthful enthusiasm.

She went through a short training period and was dispatched on her first mission . . . the mapping of the waterfront fortifications of the occupying Japanese army. She noted the locations of all enemy anti-aircraft batteries. She went in with nothing more than a sketchbook. She made her way through all the restricted areas, drawing as she saw it. Because of the drawings, American planes came attacking specific targets which she had pin-pointed for them. Their successful attacks because of her work immediately earned her the highest respect of the Allies. She was given the affectionate nickname of "Joey."

She was sent on many other difficult missions of espionage, every one was a success. Obviously, she was one brave young lady. One particularly difficult mission took her through 56 miles of Japanese-held territory. She made her way through their encampments, passed through their checkpoints, and picked her way through many of their mine fields. Meanwhile, all was accomplished with a top secret map taped to her back . . . she walked all 56 miles on foot, and returned from this, the most difficult assignment without harm, without detection, without being searched!

For more than three years, Joey kept up her undercover work. Then came the day of celebration . . . the war was over. A most grateful U.S. War Department awarded her the "Medal of Freedom" with a silver palm because of her bravery. Because of her efforts she was cited for having saved "untold" countless lives of American soldiers.

Quite a lady! But she was one of the few spies to live to tell about it. It was sort of an ultimate success story in the world of espionage. She was stopped many times by the Japanese army, but was never searched!

Why? Joey possessed a very secret weapon. This secret was a deterrent which not too many other spies would have liked to have. This was a barrier beyond which no enemy wanted to wander. It made her completely untouchable. And any enemy who wanted to search her or detain her had to deal with it. It was pretty awesome. Joey had been afflicted by a disease called: LEPROSY! And so now you know the story behind the story. Leprosy!

Here's a truth for all of us to live by: When life hands you a disaster, make the best out of it! When life, which is not always fair, hands you a lemon, make lemonade out it!

The bottom line is that the things that seem to break us are in reality the things that make us. Life is not composed of the 10 percent of things which do happen to you and me . . . but rather of the 90 percent of our reactions to the things which happen to us!

TODAY'S BIBLE READING: Joshua 2:1-24

Marion Anderson was once asked what the greatest thrill of her singing career had been. Was it singing in front of the queen of England? Was it any of her many appearances at the White House before one of the presidents? Perhaps it was singing beside Dr. Martin Luther King during his march on Washington? Or was it when she, as the very first African-American, stood in the Senate to receive the "Presidential Medal for Freedom" for her service for her country?

"No," she replied. "The greatest day of my life was when I took my mother's hands in mine and said, 'Momma, you'll never again have to take in washing.' "[13]

Children are a sacred trust given by God whether adopted or natural-born. Motives as to why children should be a part of our lives are important. There are all kinds of responsibilities which come with children.

Not the least of which is effective discipline . . . no more than the introduction of control into the life of kids. The best way in which this is accomplished is when parents live a life that demonstrates self-control and self-discipline. Here's where the old cliché comes into play: "What you are speaks so loudly I can't hear what you say." We can re-state it like this: Parents can expect no more obedience from their kids than they themselves demonstrate to the laws of God.

Let's just take one of God's commands: "Children, obey your parents in the Lord, for this is right. Honor your father and mother . . . which is the first commandment with a promise . . . that it may go well with you and that you may enjoy long life on the earth" (Eph. 6:1-3). Straightforward and simple, easily understood. But for children to learn this discipline, they must see it lived out in the lifestyle of their own parents, who also have parents.

The balance of parental relationships comes when the parents set positive examples for their own kids to follow. If a mother treats her mother with disrespect . . . the daughter will catch that example, quickly.

There is no substitute for teaching by example. The sequence is easy to follow . . . children who honor and obey their parents are motivated by parents who also demonstrate respect and honor to their own parents.

"I don't want to hear another word!"
I hear my daughter scold.
"Dear me!" I think, *She's awfully strict*
For a playful three-year-old!

She rolls her big eyes heavenward
And sighs with great disdain.
"What am I going to do with you?"
Her dolls hear her complain.

"Sit down! Be still! Hold out your hands!
Do you have to walk so slow?
Pick up your toys! Go brush your teeth!
Eat all your carrots! Blow!"

I start to tell her how gentle
A mother ought to be
When blushingly, I realize
She's imitating ME![14]

The root word for "discipline" is "discipling." To make disciples is to inspire followers. Mothers who set the example of self-discipline have kids who learn early the introduction of this control into their lives, which in turn helps them with a wonderful capability for handling the problems of life.

What happens behind the scenes, when nobody is around, is the real test of discipline. As a mother, real hope that discipline has taken is what happens when she is not there to either correct, take note of, or reward it. It has been internalized in the child; it has become a rudder that guides all of life decisions! That's the goal of discipline.

So the bottom-line admonition for motherhood has been penned by the apostle named Paul, "Be very careful, then, how you live . . . not as unwise but as wise making the most of every opportunity" (Eph. 5:15-16). Why? Because it's more than an adage that children will be like mother. Like mother, like child!

TODAY'S BIBLE READING: Ephesians 6:1-24

Helen Rosavere was an English woman from London, England, who was devoting her life to becoming a medical doctor and, in turn with her gifts and training, to serve God and humanity. Upon the completion of her medical training at Cambridge University, Helen began to ask God in prayer where He might want her to serve.

Before long, she was sensing that this commitment was directing her to an area in the Congo of Africa. The specific area had a population of more than 200,000 people without a single doctor to serve the whole area. To respond to this calling and to this area meant that she would be working seven days a week, she would always be on call, with no time off, and when facing any kind of medical problem or emergency she would have to be the one to take care of it. It would require a tremendous commitment to go . . . but she went.

She arrived and set up to begin her medical ministry. It soon became apparent that a hospital and training center was desperately needed. It was a, pressing need, but there was no way in which Helen could build it.

Helen began to pray, "Surely, Lord, there is at least one man who could come and build the hospital!"

But Helen heard nothing. No response, no one volunteered. Then, some time later, she wrote a letter to her parents back home in England asking them to find and send her a book on how to build a hospital. Her parents couldn't find a book on how to build a hospital, but they did send her a book on how to make bricks.

When the book arrived, Helen prayed again, "Surely, Lord, there is at least one man from England who could come and build bricks for the hospital." No man arrived. So . . . in the middle of Helen's busy, hectic medical schedule, she took out the book, read it, and followed the instructions. She made molds for the bricks and began making bricks for the kiln. She built the kiln and fired the bricks. After the bricks had been fired there was a remaining rough edge to be sanded down.

One day as she was sanding the hard bricks, she noticed a wet substance on the brick and realized it was her own blood. She prayed again, "Surely, Lord, there is a man somewhere who could come and make these bricks."

As she was praying, a native man came running up to Helen and shouted to her about an emergency at the dispensary. With her fingers still bleeding she went to minister to the hurting man.

When she entered the scrub room . . . she began to take a wire brush and scrub her now raw and bleeding fingers. The pain made her more irritated. She began to shout and yell at God in her spirit, "SURELY, LORD, there is at LEAST ONE MAN in all of England who could come and make bricks for the hospital!"

The attendant she had helping her began to pour alcohol over her fingers and hands to complete the sterilization. The pain was excruciating. Then Helen pulled on her surgical gloves and did what she had to do to help the injured man.

Following this emergency surgery, Helen went back out to continue working on the bricks. One of the nationals approached her and began to talk to her. He said: "Doctor, we now know that you love and care for us. When you enter the operating room wearing your mask and gown, and use your ability to heal the sick, you frighten us. But when you come out here and work with the rest of us and bleed the same as we do, we realize that you are one of us."

Dr. Helen Rosavere, then and there, for the first time, realized WHY there was no man from England who would come to help. In that moment, God whispered in her spirit, "I didn't have you come here just to heal the sick, Helen. I brought you here to befriend these people IN ORDER THAT THEY MAY SEE ME THROUGH YOU."

Helen, chastised, humbly expressed thanks to the Lord. Then it dawned on her that God didn't call her to be a medical missionary, but rather had called her to himself! Had called her to conform to the image of His Son! Had called her to let her inner light shine out for all the world to see.

In the hustle, bustle, hurt, hurry, and worry of this jostling lifestyle that you live . . . have you learned that lesson, yet?

TODAY'S BIBLE READING:
   2 Corinthians 4:1-18

28.
A LITTLE CHILD
SHALL LEAD
THEM

This took place in the church of which my father, the Rev. John M. Strand, was the pioneer, founding pastor in Mansfield, Ohio. Among the congregation was a mother and little daughter who were very faithful and consistent in church attendance. However, the father and husband wasn't interested in church. He had made it very clear that it was okay for his wife and daughter to attend but not for him. He was a steelworker, a huge hulk of a man. He could make life on his own and thank you, he didn't need God or the church in his life. All in all, quite a nice guy and a good father. The only time he attended church was when Susie was in a Christmas pageant or Easter program.

The daughter, Susie, about age six, became sick. The doctor discovered that she had leukemia and it was in an advanced stage. Techniques back then were not what they are today. The decision was to take her home and care for her as comfortably as the family could before she died. Death was expected in just a few short weeks.

Susie, being the only child, received lots of attention and loving concern from both parents as well as friends and neighbors. It became a ritual for the father . . . first thing every night on coming home from work, Susie's bedroom was her father's first stop. He would talk about his day, ask about her day, and spend lots of time with her. They played games together . . . Dad read lots of stories and did everything he could to savor the days while she was still alive.

Daily her condition worsened. She lost weight, her little cheeks became sunken, and her color was pale. It was just a matter of days, and they seemed to be flying by.

One night in particular, Susie had obviously been doing some very serious thinking and she asked her father, "Daddy, I know I will die soon and go to heaven to be with Jesus. My Sunday school teacher told me that. But, Daddy, when I get to heaven I will be given a crown to wear. And my crown will have no stars because I have not prayed with anybody to know Jesus as their Saviour. And my crown will not have any stars in it . . . so, Daddy, will you give your life to Jesus so I can have a star in my crown?"

That father, holding her hand, with tears streaming down his face, nodded his head, "Yes."

And through his tears and sobs, he simply prayed, "Lord, Jesus, I have run from You, but no more. Please forgive me my sins and my stubbornness. Come into my life. Be my Lord and Saviour . . . so Susie will have a star in her crown and so that someday I, too, can go to be with her in Your heaven." This caused Susie's eyes to light up with delight! She threw her arms around her daddy.

Together they looked up and there was Mom standing in the doorway . . . Susie told her what Daddy had just done! Talk about a happy family scene. Mom and Dad were hugging over Susie's bed, then both hugged Susie. It was one joyous happening. Then they all talked about someday meeting together in heaven . . . Mom and Dad would someday, too, catch up and go to heaven to meet Susie who had already gone on ahead. They planned that final reunion. What joy!

In just a few days, Susie passed on. Then the funeral and the final earthly farewells. On the Sunday morning following the funeral, Susie's daddy came with her mother, for the first time. Time was taken in that service for anybody to share a "testimony" of praise for the Lord. Susie's father stood and said, "May I say a few words?"

The preacher assured him, "Yes, go ahead, we'd be glad to have you testify."

The father went on, "I was resistant to the gospel and had rejected pastors and evangelists and anyone who had attempted to talk to me about Jesus Christ. I could easily reject them all, except my little daughter."

He paused to wipe the tears away and went on, "But because she asked and because she loved me, I gave my life to Jesus. She reached me when no one else could." Just before he sat down, he looked upward and finished with this: "And now Susie is in heaven, wearing the crown promised to her with a single star in her crown . . . and that star is me!"

Who is there in your life, in your circle of friends, that you could be instrumental in directing and leading into a new lifestyle, a new relationship with the Creator of this world? Who can only you influence with your love?

TODAY'S BIBLE READING: Luke 15:1-32

29.
IN THE GOOD
OLD DAYS

This meditation is dedicated to those mothers among us who have a few years of life behind them. If it's okay with you younger ones, please let the older moms get just a bit nostalgic for today. Okay? Well, ready or not, here goes. . . .

IN THE GOOD OLD DAYS

Grandmother, on a winter's day,
Milked the cows, and fed them hay,
Slopped the hogs, saddled the mule,
And got the children off to school.

Did a washing, mopped the floors,
Washed the windows, and did some chores.
Cooked a dish of home-dried fruit,
Pressed her husband's Sunday suit

Swept the parlor, made the bed,
Baked a dozen loaves of bread,
Split some firewood, and lugged in
Enough to fill the kitchen bin.
Cleaned the lamps, and put in oil,

Stewed some apples she thought might spoil.
Churned the butter, baked a cake,
Then exclaimed, "For goodness sake
The calves have got out of the pen,"
Went out and chased them in again.

Gathered the eggs, and locked the stable,
Back to the house and set the table.
Cooked a supper that was delicious,
And after washed up all the dishes.

Fed the cat and sprinkled the clothes,
Mended a basket full of hose;
Then opened the organ and began to play
"When You Come to the End of a Perfect Day."

(Author is unknown)

While we're on this nostalgic kick, let's take it a bit further, and continue to wallow some more in the past. Just consider. . . .

IF YOU WERE BORN BEFORE 1945 . . .

Consider some of the changes we have witnessed: We were born before television, penicillin, polio shots, frozen foods, Xerox, plastic, contact lenses, frisbees, the pill, radar, credit cards, split atoms, laser beams, ball-point pens, pantyhose, dishwashers, clothes dryers, electric blankets, air conditioners, water beds, drip-dry clothes, wrinkle-free clothes, computers, and before anyone walked on the moon!

We got married first and then lived together! How quaint can you be?

In our time, closets were for clothes, not for "coming out of," bunnies were small rabbits, and rabbits were not Volkswagens. Designer jeans were scheming girls named Jean or Jeanne and having a meaningful relationship meant getting along well with our cousins.

We thought fast food was what you ate during Lent and outer space was the back of the Bijou Theater. We were before house-husbands, gay rights, animal rights, or anybody's rights, computer dating, dual careers, day care centers, group therapy, and nursing homes. We never heard of FM radio, tape decks, CDs, cellular phones, artificial hearts, word processors, yogurt, or guys wearing earrings. For us . . . time-sharing meant togetherness, not computers or condominiums; a "chip" meant a piece of wood; hardware meant screws and nails, and software wasn't even a word!

In 1940, "Made in Japan" meant junk and the term "making out" referred to how you did on your exam. Pizzas, McDonalds, Burger King, and instant coffee were unheard of.

We hit the scene when there were five and dime stores, where you actually bought things for five and ten cents. Snelgrove's or Farr's or Bridgman's sold ice cream cones for a nickel or a dime for two dips. For one nickel you could ride a streetcar, make a phone call, buy a coke or enough stamps to mail one letter and two post cards. You could buy a new Chevy coupe for $600, but who could afford one? A pity, too, because gas was 11 cents a gallon!

In our day grass was mowed, coke was a cold soft drink, and pot was something you cooked in.

Rock music was Grandma's lullaby and aids were helpers.

We were certainly not before the difference between the sexes was discovered but we were surely before the sex change operation; we had to make do with what we had. And, we were the last generation that was so dumb as to think you needed a husband to have a baby!

No wonder we are confused and that there is such a generation gap today.

But, somehow, we all survived!

And what better reason is there to celebrate?

However . . . come to think of it, maybe the "good-old-days" weren't so good after all. Just how could we ever survive without kleenex, soaps, de-caf coffee, waterbeds, phone cards, ATMs, micro-wave popcorn, or reality sessions?

Are we to live in the past or in the future? Are we to be controlled by the past or run toward the future? We are accustomed to thinking, "past . . . present . . . future." Which brings to mind something interesting to contemplate: Should we view time as flowing from the future into the present and then into the past? or should time be viewed as flowing from our past into the present and then on to the future? Interesting!

I submit, that if you are a believer . . . you should be future-oriented! Time flows from the future to the present to be forgotten as we move ahead. The apostle Paul wrote, "But one thing I do: FORGETTING what is behind and straining toward what is ahead, I press on" (Phil. 3:13). Please keep in mind that this Bible word, "forgetting" doesn't mean "to fail to remember." And apart from becoming senile, or under hypnosis, or having a brain malfunction, no mature person can forget what has happened in the past. We may wish we could, but we can't.

However, "forgetting" in the Bible sense, and taken from the original Greek language in which the Bible was written, the "forgetting" here means that we will "no longer be influenced or affected by what is in the past!" This forgetting the past is an impossible feat of mental gymnastics by which we can erase the past. It means that by the grace of God we break the power of the past by living for the future. None of us can change the past . . . but we can change the meaning of the past. God came to set us free from the shackles of the past. "Whom the Son sets free is free indeed!" (John 8:36)

Don't be shackled by regrets of the past. Not only the failures — we can also be distracted by the successes of the past which can be just as bad. "What is behind" must be set aside so that "what is ahead" takes its place!

The good old days or the best is yet to come? Which shall it be?

Let's close this message by a prayer:

Dear Heavenly Father . . . I, for the first time, realize how I have been influenced by the events of my past. Please forgive me, I have been living in the past, I have been influenced by my past, I have guided the present too much by the past. In the name of Your Son, Jesus Christ, set me free from the bondage of the past. From this moment on, with your help, I shall move from the past into the future with faith. Help me to do the same as the Apostle who positively moved into the future, because that's where my eternal home will be. From this moment on I will look to You, I will set my sights on Jesus Christ, I will look up and look ahead rather than keep turning to the past. Thank You for hearing me. I pray it in the name of Your Son. AMEN!

TODAY'S BIBLE READING: Philippians 3:1-21

30.
GEMS JUST
FOR MOM

When writing a book like this, an author comes across lots of little tidbits that are wonderful, but that just don't quite seem to fit into anything else. Some of these I've collected into a potpourri of bits and pieces which I hope you will enjoy:

I'LL NEVER TELL

A mother and daughter drove to a special shopping mall about 35 miles away. They had a wonderful time shopping. But when it came to leave, they discovered that the keys were locked in the car. They didn't know what to do, but called back home to the husband. Understandably, he was a bit upset.

A few minutes later, the teenage daughter tried one of the back doors. Sure enough, one was unlocked! The mother rushed back into the mall, hoping to reach her husband before he left, but it was too late. She returned to the car and she told the daughter that she had just missed him. "Wait until dad sees this!" she said. "He'll be more than a little upset. What are you going to do?"

"What any red-blooded American would do," she replied, grinning. Then she walked over to the car, opened the door, pushed down the lock button and slammed it shut! With the keys still inside!

EARLY SIGNS OF LOVE

One morning, my son came down to breakfast looking especially handsome in a color-coordinated outfit. Just one thing was wrong . . . his collar was twisted. "You look great," I said, reaching to straighten his collar.

He said, "No, Mom. Please don't. When I see a certain person in history class, she will arrange it for me."

(Patty McGinley)

MOTHERLY LOVE . . .

Is that unexplainable emotion causing her to save the choice piece of meat for the kids, or to take the other egg because it wasn't fried just right, or wear the same old dress another year so she can have a formal for the prom, or sit in a cold car in the schoolyard until 3:00 a.m. waiting for the bus to bring them back from an out-of-town ballgame.

COMMUNICATION IS THE KEY TO A HAPPY MARRIAGE

A golden anniversary party was thrown for an elderly couple. The husband was emotionally moved by the occasion and wanted to tell his wife just how he felt about her. She was very hard of hearing, however, and often misunderstood what was said. With many family members and friends gathered around, he toasted her: "My dear wife, after 50 years I've found you tried and true!"

Everyone smiled approval, but the wife said, "Ehhh?"

He repeated, louder this time: "AFTER 50 YEARS I'VE FOUND YOU TRIED AND TRUE!"

His wife harumphed and shot back, "Well, let me tell you something . . . after 50 years I'm tired of you, too!"

THE UNIQUE SEND-OFF

When Corrine Hicks emerged with her newlywed husband, after the wedding had taken place at St. Paul's Church in Wodinham, England, her father released 2,000 beautiful butterflies on the church steps. This labor of love had been in process for more than a year. He began cultivating the butterflies in a spare room of their home a year before . . . when he had learned that confetti and rice was banned for use at weddings at that church.

A CHILD'S PERSPECTIVE

A little boy was talking to the little girl next door: "I wonder what my mother would like for Mother's Day."

The little girl answers: "Well, you could promise to keep your room clean and orderly . . . you could go to bed as soon as she tells you . . . you could go to her as soon as she calls you . . . you could brush your teeth after eating . . . you could quit fighting with your brothers and sisters, especially at the dinner table."

The little boy looked at her and replied: "No . . . I mean something practical."

APPRECIATING MOTHER

Not until I became a mother did I understand how much my mother had sacrificed for me; not until I became a mother did I feel how hurt my mother was when I disobeyed; not until I became a mother did I know how proud my mother was when I achieved; not until I became a mother did I realize how much my mother loves me.

(Victoria Farnsworth)

THE STORK STORY STRIKES AGAIN

A little boy asked his mother where he came from and also where she had come from as a baby. His mother gave him the old tall tale about a beautiful white-feathered bird. The boy ran into the next room and asked his grandmother the same question and received a variation on the same old stork story. He then ran outside to one of his friends and made this comment: "You know, there hasn't been a normal birth in our family for three generations!"

THE WEAK LINK

In ancient China, the people desired security from the barbaric hordes to the north, so they built the "Great Wall of China." It was so high they knew no one could climb over it, and so thick that nothing could break it down. They settled back to enjoy their security. During the first one hundred years of the wall's existence, China was invaded three times! Not once did the barbaric hordes break down the wall or climb over the top. Each time they bribed a gatekeeper and marched right through the gate. The Chinese people were so busy relying on the walls of stone that they forgot to teach integrity to the children who grew up to guard the gates.

A CHILD IS LISTENING

One day as a young mother and her kindergarten-aged son were driving down the street, his little head was turning frantically from side to side. His mother finally asked him what he was doing. He said, "I'm looking for all those blooming idiots who always come out when Daddy drives!"

RETROSPECTIVE

A little girl was looking through one of the family picture albums. She came across the pictures of her mom and dad on their wedding day. She carried the album over to where her father was reading the paper and asked, "Daddy, is this the day you got mom to come and work for us?"

TODAY'S BIBLE READING: Proverbs 14:1-35

31.
MORE GEMS
JUST FOR MOMS

MOTHER . . .

I think it was a girlish hand,
Unlined, well-tended, when it held
At first, my clinging baby hand
In gentle grasps by love impelled.

I think it was a youthful face
That bent above me as I lay
Asleep, and bright the eyes that watched
My rest, in that forgotten day.

I think it was a slender form
That bore my weight on tiring arm,
And swift young feet that watched my steps
To guide them from the ways of harm.

But years and cares have changed that form
And face and hand; have streaked with gray
The hair; yet is the heart as full
Of love as in that other day.

And she has her reward; not fame, or baubles bought in any mart,
But motherhood's brave crown, the love and homage of her own child's heart.

(Author is unknown)

RECIPE FOR MOTHERS

Pre-heat oven . . . check for rubber balls or plastic ninja men who might have been lurking inside. Clear counter of wooden blocks and any hot-wheels cars. Grease pan. Crack nuts. Measure flour . . . remove Jimmy's hands from flour. Re-measure flour. Crack more nuts to replace those Jimmy has just eaten.

Sift flour, baking powder, and salt. Get broom and dustpan. Sweep up pieces of bowl Jimmy knocked on the floor, accidentally. Find a second mixing bowl. Answer doorbell.

Return to kitchen. Remove Jimmy's hands from bowl. Wash Jimmy. Answer phone. Remove one-half inch of salt from greased pan. Call for Jimmy. Look for Jimmy. Give up on search. Grease another pan. Answer phone.

Return to kitchen and find Jimmy. Remove Jimmy's hands from bowl. Remove layer of nut shells from greased pan. Sternly turn to Jimmy . . . who knocks the second bowl off counter while attempting to get away. Wash kitchen floor, counter, cupboards, stove, dishes, and walls.

Final scene: Call the bakery and order a cake. Tuck Jimmy into bed for a nap. Take two aspirin. Lie down.

THE DOMINATION OF LOVE

It is early morning before breakfast when a youngster walks onto a newly cleaned floor with muddy feet, hands behind his back. Just as mother, who stayed up last night to clean, was about to get angry the boy brings his hands from behind his back with a bunch of wild flowers he just picked, saying: "It's your birthday, Mommy, Happy Birthday!"

Now, how many mothers would say, "What's the big idea tracking dirt onto my clean floor!" Not many. It would be more like, "Thank you for remembering that, sweetheart," and then CARRY him out of the room! That's what perfect love is all about. God isn't looking down saying, "Ah-ha, a bit of mud on the shoe there I see!" No . . . God's love dominates us. Sure, we make mistakes, but does it really matter, if we're dominated by the love of God?

(Dr. Donald English, British scholar)

A CHILD'S VIEW OF LOVE

Some children were asked: "What is love?"

One little girl answered, "Love is when your mommy reads you a bedtime story. TRUE LOVE is when she doesn't skip any pages."

THE COMPANY WE KEEP

A mother was quite concerned about her only son going off to college. She wrote the following letter to the college president:

Dear Sir: My son has been accepted for admission to your college and soon he will be leaving me. I am writing to ask that you give your personal attention to the selection of his roommate. I want to be sure that his roommate is not the kind of person who uses foul language, or tells off-color stories, smokes, drinks, or chases after girls. I hope you will understand why I am appealing to you directly. You see, this is the first time my son will be away from home, except for his four years in the Marine Corps.

TYPECASTING

After many years of hauling children, pets, groceries, little league ball teams, and camping gear, the family station wagon finally gave up the ghost, stopped, and refused to go any further. My wife told me she was ready for a change in cars . . . but I didn't realize how large a change until we were inside the car dealer's showroom. There she fell madly in love with one of those snazzy foreign sports cars.

I pointed out, "But, honey, this eight-passenger van over here has power steering, luggage rack, fold-down seats, anti-lock brakes for the same price as the sports car."

She glared resentfully at the van, then snapped, "I just don't like it!"

"But . . . why not?"

"Because it has 'MOTHER' written all over it!"

TODAY'S BIBLE READING: Psalm 141:1-10

32.
ADD TO YOUR
LIFE...KINDNESS!

One family, who had emigrated from Japan at the turn of this century and settled near San Francisco, had established a business in which they grew roses and trucked them into the city three mornings a week. There is another family, who had come from Switzerland, who also grew and sold roses in the same market. Both families, who were neighbors, had become modestly successful. Their secret of success in the San Francisco markets was that their roses were known for their long vase-life.

For almost four decades the two families had run the businesses which were now turned over to their sons to farm. It was an ideal, wonderful lifestyle. But all that changed when on December 7, 1941, Japan bombed Pearl Harbor. All of the original family members had become naturalized U.S. citizens, except the father of the Japanese family. There was turmoil and lots of questions about internment camps being a real possibility. The Switzerland family father assured the Japanese father that, if necessary, he would look after his friend's nursery and business. It was something each family had learned in life and from the teachings of their church: LOVE YOUR NEIGHBOR AS YOURSELF. "You would do the same for us," he told his Japanese friend.

It wasn't long before the Japanese family was transported to the barren landscape of Granada, Colorado. The relocation/internment camp consisted of plain tarpaper-roofed barracks surrounded by barbed wire and armed guards.

A full year went by, then two, and then three. While the Japanese neighbors were in this internment, their neighbors worked in the greenhouses and the fields. The children helped before and after school with the father's work days sometimes stretching to 16 or 18 hours. Then . . . one day, when the war ended, the Japanese family packed up their few belongings and boarded a train to return home.

They were met at the depot by their neighbors and when they got to their farm, the whole Japanese family could only stare, stunned! There was the nursery intact, scrubbed, and shining in the California sunshine. It was neat, prosperous, and healthy!

Then they went into the house which was just as clean and welcoming as the nursery had been. So was the balance in the bank passbook handed to the Japanese father. And there on the dining room table was ONE perfect red rosebud . . . just waiting to unfold, the gift of one neighbor to another! (adapted, story by Diane Rayner)

Dr. Karl Menninger once said: "Love cures people . . . both the ones who give it and the ones who receive it."

The apostle Peter has distilled for us the very essence of what Christian living is all about in 2 Peter 1:3-11. We are looking at only one of these special character qualities: "Brotherly kindness." In the original Greek language, this is a word we know about, "philadelphian" love. It is a fraternal affection, fondness for another person in the family of God or a person outside the family of God. It's to be shown to all people.

I suspect that this was a quality of character that Peter must have acquired the hard way. If we read the records in the Gospels, we discover that often the disciples of Jesus were given to debate and disagreement. In fact, later, from the Book of Acts we can read about a public confrontation Paul had with Peter. It's the quality of life which is to distinguish us from people who are not a part of the family of God. By this quality of love and kindness, all others will know that we are disciples, followers of Jesus Christ. We find this truth in many places in the Bible. This, when manifested, gives credence to the fact that we have become a new creation because of what Jesus Christ has completed in our hearts.

The concern of Peter is that we become responsible to the development and growth of this discipline. We are responsible to make sure that "kindness" is added to the other graces of our living. Not always easy, but oh so necessary.

Relationships are absolutely crucial for the Christian! We have become members of the most important family in the universe. Therefore, we must not, cannot, ignore this function. If we do ignore it, we become weak and non-productive.

This society in which we live is less and less influenced by even the smallest measures of common grace and neighborly courtesy. For too many people, it has become a hateful place in which to live. BUT what an opportunity for you and me to live out a contrasting lifestyle! Our lives, by their difference, denote a different moral value system. We who believe in a personal relationship with Jesus Christ should be taking steps to re-introduce kindness into society in these days. How?

FIRST . . . REMEMBER THAT WE BELONG TO EACH OTHER. We are members of a special family called the "body of Christ," and as such we are the visible representation of that relationship here on this earth (Eph. 1:22-23). We are told how this is to be lived out (Eph. 4:1-6). We are to work together in order to become united (Eph. 4:12-13). We are to express that wonderful sense of belonging (Heb. 10:24-25). We are told to do good to others (Gal. 6:10). And, we are called to not abuse anybody else (Gal. 5:13-15). So, what is really important in life?

This allegedly happened at the Seattle Special Olympics. There were nine contestants who all were physically or mentally disabled assembling at the starting line for the 100-yard dash. All were excited, all were eager, and all had trained for this special moment.

When the gun sounded, all jumped from the starting line with a desire to be a winner. All that is, except one young man who tripped and fell to the track and tumbled to his back . . . and he began to cry. They all slowed, paused, turned around, and went back. All of them! One girl with Down's syndrome bent over and kissed him and said, "This will make it all better."

They helped him to his feet . . . then all nine linked arms with each other and walked together across the finish line!

There's a life principle here: Nobody crosses the finish line until we ALL cross it together and "Philadelphian" love makes it a reality!

SECOND . . . PURPOSELY PERFORM AN ACT OF KINDNESS FOR ANOTHER. Have you ever, when traveling through a toll booth, paid the toll for the car following behind you? Have you ever done a special act of kindness for another, anonymously? Have you ever put yourself out at some considerable cost in order to help another?

This being a healthy human being is dependent upon lots of things and lots of people. Consider this: Virginia Satir has made a study of acts of kindness and their effects on people. She came to this conclusion: "We need four hugs a day for survival. We need eight hugs a day for maintenance. We need twelve hugs a day for growth!"

Millions of people in today's world know only hatred, vindictiveness, mistrust, anger, hurt, and disappointment. The kindness of a Christian can be the very key that allows us to make a difference. How about waking each morning with this assignment for the day: WHAT ACT OF KINDNESS COULD I DO TODAY FOR A PERSON WHO NEEDS ME?

We'll continue with this same subject in the next chapter. . . .

TODAY'S BIBLE READING: 2 Peter 1:3-21

The cartoon strip, "Momma" has the son running up and saying, "Hi, Momma! Can you sew on this button, in a hurry? And iron these slacks? And give me a cold glass of water? Thanks, Momma. Got to run!"

In the last frame, Momma looks at him leaving and sighs, "In the 'Indy 500' of life, mothers are the pit stops."

So it seems, too often. Battle lines have been drawn early in human history for one of the major conflicts of this age. Let's go back to the origins of history to read, "And I will put enmity between you (Satan) and the woman, and between your offspring and hers; he will crush your head, and you will strike his heel" (Gen. 3:15).

Through a woman, Mary, came the Saviour of the world into this world. Not only did Jesus come . . . but as that prophecy said, "He will crush your head" in a defeat of Satan for all times which took place on Calvary. Satan is a defeated foe! And a woman was the channel or vessel through which this became a possibility.

In order to stop this invasion of his territory, Satan let loose a spirit of murder in the world with King Herod killing all the boy babies at the time of Christ's birth. Is this the reason we have much the same kind of a spirit let loose to take from this world the offspring of women through abortion? Just think of the millions worldwide who have been deprived of life before birth! How many of these could have been the scientist who unlocked some of the secrets of conquering disease? In the United States, think of the millions who have been taken from our tax roles, taken from productivity, robbed of their contributions in many, many ways in making this a better world in which to live.

This battle line has been drawn through history and blatantly or subtly women have been put in their place! And sad to say, too often, the Church, has been playing a major role in this subjugation. Look around you . . . at every turn, destruction is targeted at women. Conflicts in broken marriages, putting down the role of the homemaker-mother, making the woman's role of little or no importance. There are attacks being waged which portray women as sex objects in our pornographic world. There are attacks on the self-esteem of women. But I believe that God is in the process of raising up a great army of godly women to show the character of God to this world!

A small boy was sitting with his mother in church, listening to the sermon entitled, "What is a Christian?" The minister punctuated his talk by asking, "What is a Christian?" Each time, he pounded his fist on the pulpit for emphasis.

At one point, the lad whispered to his mother, "Momma, do you know? Do you know what a Christian is?"

"Yes, dear," his mother replied, "now try to sit still and listen."

As the minister was wrapping up the sermon, once more he thundered, "What is a Christian?" and he pounded extra hard on the pulpit for his emphasis.

At that, the boy jumped up and shouted, "Tell him, Momma, tell him!"

WOMEN ARE LIFE-BEARERS!

When God created woman . . . He created her with certain gifts and sensitivities that men possess to a lesser degree. These traits are needed because women were created to be the life-bringers, life-bearers, and the nurturers. It's vitally important that women are allowed to bring these womanly qualities into every area of life. The whole fabric of society needs to be touched by the qualities that women possess! The world would be a much better place in which to live!

Our former president George Bush talked about building a "gentler, kinder" nation and world. Women could help bring that about. If we had only women in national leadership, do you think this world would be in the mess it's in today? Homes need you, churches need you, this nation needs you, this world needs you!

But Satan has diverted that. Women have been relegated to positions of less importance in the eyes of the world. Satan has told women that men are the only ones doing important work. Child-raising and homemaking are viewed as lesser occupations. This enemy has convinced women to go so far as to model themselves after men, to be a success in this world. Many have denied their God-given womanhood.

Let's take one issue: ABORTION! Women were created to be life-bearers. Now the world is trying to tell women that it is actually noble for a woman to discard the fruit of her womb. She is simply exercising her "right to choose." What happens to women who opt for this action even though a mother's basic instinct is to protect her young? Such action does violence to the inner personhood of a woman.

Without women . . . where would our churches be today? They basically have been the teachers, the prayer warriors, and the faithful ones in attendance. For verification just check out any typical church audience on any given Sunday morning worship service. The women outnumber the men. The women are the ones doing most of the work of ministry . . . but men have taken the leadership positions as well as most of the credit.

In the economy and plan of God . . . there is to be NO distinction in the family of God! Read it again, "There is neither Jew nor Greek, slave nor free, MALE NOR FEMALE, FOR YOU ARE ALL ONE IN CHRIST JESUS. If you belong to Christ, then you are Abraham's seed and heirs according to the promise" (Gal. 3:28-29). Here it's stated for all time . . . in God's plan all racial differences come down, all class distinctions are to fall, and all sexual barriers are to be put aside! Because of Jesus Christ, we all stand on the same level. And, ladies, I'm sorry to have to tell you that too often, churches, who should be leading the way in practicing this equality, have only given token agreement.

Madam . . . stand tall in the freedom that has been purchased for you! Jesus Christ has come to set us free from bondage. In the physical sense, women are life-bearers and in the spiritual sense, as well!

There was a Mother's Day card that I once read, with this inscription: "Now that we have a mature, adult relationship, there's something I'd like to tell you. You're still the first person I think of when I fall down and go boom!"

Motherhood is extremely important in the plan of God! And your relationship with God elevates all of womanhood to the place of equality where there are no distinctions to be made.

Congratulations . . . you now know WHO you are! You are highly valued by GOD!

TODAY'S BIBLE READING:
Galatians 3:15-4:7

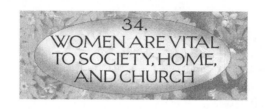

The bias against women is seen everywhere, especially in our humor. For example: They keep saying women are smarter than men . . . but have you ever seen any kind of men's clothing that buttons or zips up the back?

Or . . . I'm glad there is sexual equality in all areas today. Just this morning my wife was discussing this very issue with her Avon man. How about this? Yes . . . I'm writing a book about men's liberation, it'll be published just as soon as my wife okays it.

Yeah, we laugh . . . but even humor can sting with a hidden barb. Let me say it again: WOMEN HAVE SPECIAL GIFTS AND CHARACTERISTICS THAT MAKE THEM DANGEROUS TO SATAN, BUT VITAL TO SOCIETY, HOME, AND CHURCH! Consider the following areas of living in which women have proven time and time again just how vital they really are:

1) WOMEN DO NOT EASILY GIVE UP! Every time I read Luke 18:1-6 I just have to chuckle. Jesus is challenging His disciples about praying and never giving up, "They [men, disciples] should always pray and not give up!" Then . . . to illustrate this challenge, Jesus uses an illustration featuring a woman with these characteristics! Why a woman? Perhaps there were no "men" illustrations which came to His mind. Don't tell me that Jesus didn't have a sense of humor.

Women know intuitively how to be persistent! It has been discovered in studies that if the husband is an alcoholic in a marriage that 90 percent of the women will stay with their mate. However, if we reverse the situation and the woman is the alcoholic of the spouses, 90 percent of the men will eventually leave their alcoholic wife. The tables are completely reversed.

The woman was not originally created to darn socks, fix meals, wash clothes, chauffeur kids. She was made to communicate with the man, on an equal basis! But when trouble comes into a marriage, the first thing to disappear is communication and openness to each and God. And this seems to be the major area of attack on our homes.

Other women illustrate this truth of being persistent. Consider the lady with the issue of blood. She did an action which was strictly forbidden by law in public. She pressed through the crowd and didn't give up until she had touched the hem of His garment! She said within herself, *If I can but touch the hem of His garment, I shall be made whole.* In spite of pain or rejection or other obstacles, she kept on her mission until she touched Him! Women don't easily give up!

2) WOMEN TEND TO EXPRESS IT WHEN THEY HAVE BEEN TOUCHED BY GOD! The woman in question was indeed a questionable character . . . five husbands and now a live-in relationship. But she is featured in 42 verses dedicated to her from the Gospel of John. When she had experienced the living water . . . she left her water jug and went back into her town and many of the inhabitants were influenced by her to also "believe in Him." Why? "Because of the woman's testimony!"

You get enough women excited and turned on to the things of God and they will make a difference in our churches and in our communities! Ladies, let's begin to harness this tremendous possibility for God. When God has done something special for you . . . share it!

3) WOMEN ARE MUCH MORE WILLING TO MAKE SACRIFICES! Mary, with a single gift, "about a pint of pure nard, an expensive perfume" poured it out over the feet of Jesus without being asked. How costly was this gift? Judas Iscariot said, "It was worth a year's wages!" Women tend to be more generous and sacrificial in their giving than men. Women tend to be less concerned about the personal cost in life, in shopping, in giving, in worship, in parenting.

Every night when the mother tucked her daughter in bed, the little girl said, "Mommy, your hair is beautiful. I love your hair. Mommy, your eyes are beautiful, I love your eyes. Mommy, your face is beautiful, I love your face. But Mommy, your arms are ugly. I cannot love your arms."

One night when the mother was again tucking in her little girl, she told her daughter that once when the daughter had been a tiny baby, there had been a fire and the mother had reached through the flames to lift and carry the little girl to safety.

The daughter was quiet for a long minute or two . . . then, "Mommy, your hair is beautiful, I love it. Mommy, your eyes and your face are beautiful. I love them. But Mommy, your arms are the most beautiful of them all and I love them the bestest!"

Women are most willing to sacrifice. When they take on another job, they stretch themselves, even to losing sleep to do it. Men? Well, I hate to admit it, but we tend to pick and choose, it becomes an either/or situation for us. Men will drop something off their list. Men have been raised to be "takers" and women have been socialized to be the "givers" in life. When she takes on something else as duty . . . first she'll give up her free time and then her sleep to get it all done.

When pastoring a church in St. Joseph, Missouri, we were taking a "Giant Killer" offering so that a new building could be built. We had outgrown the present facility. I watched as the plates were being passed down one of the side sections. One of the plates slowed as it went by Bev and a small commotion took place, then the offering place continued on its way. Later I found out that she had taken the diamond ring from her finger and placed it in the plate as her sacrificial offering. About $32,000 was received in that offering, including the diamond ring which was sold and the money given. It became a rally point for further offerings . . . that diamond in the offering plate!

Let's harness this beautiful trait for making differences in this world!

4) WOMEN HAVE A GREATER TENDENCY TO STICK TO SOMETHING TO THE END! Who were the last people gathered at the foot of the cross when Jesus died? Who were the first ones at the empty tomb on resurrection Sunday? Who stood by when all the others fled in fear? Who was the first person to whom Jesus spoke to after His resurrection? Who had to go with a message that He lives to His hiding disciples? Who never lost hope? Who never lost faith? Who never gave up? The answer to all the "who" questions: a woman or women!

Take a simple thing like "pregnancy" . . . the man was there to start the process, but from then, it's God and the mother. Sometimes she may wish to back out, but that is commitment!

5) WOMEN WILL RISE TO THE CHALLENGE IN TIMES OF CRISIS! The beautiful Queen Esther is one prime example of this trait. She was willing to give her life to help her people and even sacrifice her

own life to save their life, if necessary. Godly women are just like that today. Women will march on the battle against pornography, make their appeals before school boards, confront library boards, challenge city councils, picket abortion clinics, and even run for office in order to make this a better world in which their children can live, can mature in.

One pastor's wife tells the following: "Shortly after our son had assumed the pastorate of his first church, he and his wife came to visit us. I sensed that she was a bit unhappy; not wishing to be a meddlesome mother-in-law, I pretended not to notice. But as they departed, I overheard her say: 'All right, we will go by the church one more time and you can practice baptizing me just once more. But remember this . . . when you have your first funeral, you are not going to practice burying me!' "

BECAUSE she understood me better far than I myself could understand;
Because her faith in me, like a guiding star, steadied my feet, and strengthened heart and hand.
Because her cheer and tender sympathy were strewn along the stony path she trod;
Because of her underlying love for me, I better comprehend the love of God.

(Author is unknown)

The lady was small, old, and frail. She had lost the sight of one of her eyes and it had to be removed. When it was to be replaced with a false eye, she said to her doctor, "Be sure to choose one with a twinkle in it."

Women today are coming to the forefront in many different walks of life. Wonderful! Find an area of ministry fits you . . . and get with the program!

TODAY'S BIBLE READING:
Luke 18:1-6; John 4:1-42

35.
HAVE YOU THOUGHT ABOUT BEING "GOOD"?

Danny Sutton wrote this for his third grade Sunday school teacher, who had asked her students to explain God:

One of God's main jobs is making people. He makes these to put in place of the ones who die so there will be enough people to take care of things here on earth.

He doesn't make grownups, He just makes babies. I think because they are smaller and easier to make. That way He doesn't have to take up His valuable time teaching them to walk and talk. He can just leave that up to the mothers and fathers. I think it works out pretty good.

God's second most important job is listening to prayers. An awful lot of this goes on, cause some people, like preachers and things, pray other times besides bedtimes, and Grandpa and Grandma pray every time they eat, except for snacks.

God sees and hears everything and is everywhere, which keeps Him pretty busy. So you shouldn't go wasting His time asking for things that aren't important, or go over parents' heads and ask for something they said you couldn't have. It doesn't work anyway.

Sounds to me as though eight-year-old Danny has just about got it right "God's main job is making people!" Okay, then, so how does God go about making people "good"? It's a process in which we have an active part to play. The apostle Peter writes "For this very reason, [YOU' is implied] make every effort to add to your faith GOODNESS"! (2 Pet. 1:5). It sounds good . . . but how do we go about doing this?

What is "goodness," as used here? This particular word from the original Greek language is a very rare word in biblical Greek, but it was used quite frequently in non-Christian writings. It means "excellence" and can also be translated as "virtue" or you can simply take it as it was written, goodness.

The meaning is expanded when we understand it to mean that the excellence of a knife is to cut; the excellence of a race horse is to run; the best thing a Christian can do is to become Christ-like in character.

What really is the excellence of motherhood? Let's take a look at three aspects of goodness.

At bedtime, Lillian Holcomb told her two grandsons a Bible story, then asked if they knew what the word "sin" meant. Seven-year-old Keith spoke up: "It's when you do something real bad."

Four-year-old Aaron's eyes widened and he said: "I know a big sin Keith did today."

Annoyed, Keith turned to his brother: "You take care of your sins and I'll take care of mine!"

Precisely . . . it is our responsibility, yours and mine, to do something about being good in every sense of the word. Consider, then:

GOODNESS AS GOODNESS: The Bible is the best commentary on the Bible, so we turn to the Bible to understand and build an awareness as to our subject at hand.

Barnabas, in Acts 11:24, is described as "a good man, full of the Holy Spirit and faith." Also, here is one clue as to the "how" question. You, too, must open your life to the fullness of the Holy Spirit and faith.

"Well done, GOOD and faithful servant. You have been faithful with a few things; I will put you in charge of many things" (Matt. 25:21). Another clue . . . to be good is to be faithful, consistent, to be counted on. Also to be a good steward or manager of the gifts and talents given to you. Character is revealed by successful servanthood in this story.

"The GOOD woman (man) brings GOOD things out of the GOOD stored up in her (him) and the evil person brings evil things out of the evil stored up inside" (Matt. 12:35). Here's another how-to-do-it principle. "Store" up good things inside. Fill the gaps and voids in the mind, heart, and soul with good things to think on, to meditate on. From the computer world we have the "GIGO" principle . . . "garbage in equals garbage out." No computer is better than the programming. No person can be better than what is on the inside.

"Salt is GOOD, but if it loses its saltiness, how can you make it salty again? Have salt in yourselves"

(Mark 9:50). Salt becomes the example of what good people are and do. Salt flavors all that comes in contact with it. Good people are the flavor in society. To forfeit that flavor is to be good for nothing and is to be thrown out. There is nothing so useless as salt without salt. "Have salt in yourselves."

"We pray this in order that you may live a life worthy of the Lord and may please Him in every way: bearing fruit in every GOOD work, growing in the knowledge of God" (Col. 1:10). Here's the process . . . like growing fruit. The seed is planted, cultivated, watered, fertilized, pruned until good fruit appears. The seed of goodness has been planted inside each of us when we became Christians . . . now it's our responsibility to help the process of maturing to be ongoing. A good life, full of good deeds, coming out of a good heart is Christ-like in the best sense.

Jesus replied, "There is only One who is GOOD" (Matt. 19:17). And that is the fountainhead from which all goodness comes. God is good! God is love! Therefore the more of God I have in my life, the more I manifest goodness.

Here is the bottom line challenge, "Live such GOOD lives among the pagans that, though they accuse you of doing wrong, they may see your GOOD deeds and glorify God on the day He visits you" (1 Pet. 2:12). Quite simply . . . Christianity needs good people, society needs good people, and the Church needs good people.

A four-year-old girl is at her pediatrician's office for her regular checkup. As the doctor looked into her ears with an otoscope, he asked, "Do you think I'll find Big Bird in here?" She remained silent.

Next, the doctor took a tongue depressor and looked down her throat and asked, "Do you think I'll find the Cookie Monster down there?" Again, she was silent.

Then the doctor put a stethoscope to her chest and as he listened to her heart beat, he asked, "Do you think I'll hear Barney in here?"

"Oh, no!" she replied, "Jesus is in my heart. Barney's on my underpants!"

And our world is asking, "where is Jesus?" Well, He's living in my heart is our standard answer. But is the goodness of God being manifested in life-actions which will be translated as a life of good deeds bringing glory to God?

 TODAY'S BIBLE READING: 1 Peter 2:1-12

36.
HAVE YOU THOUGHT ABOUT BEING "GOOD"?

(PART II)

Linda Chavez, former executive director of the U.S. Commission on Civil Rights, says: "Historically, virtually all societies have condemned incest, adultery, and homosexuality because such practices, in distinctive ways, threaten the family. Over the past 25 years, we have become increasingly tolerant of sexually permissive behavior. But that tolerance has had consequences. We face epidemics in sexually transmitted diseases, teenage pregnancies, abortions, illegitimacy, rape, and sexual abuse. Marriage rates are on the decline and divorce is on the increase, especially among younger couples. The American family may not yet be an endangered species, but it is far from thriving."

As we continue where we left off in our last message, let's first look at . . .

GOODNESS AS VIRTUE: Virtue is selling today. It's become a political hot-potato, and we all hope that it begins to make a difference. Diverse people such as Bennett, Quayle, Hillary Clinton, and Pipher all have written and are peddling books on virtue.

According to the Greeks, the word "virtue" meant when anything fulfilled its purpose, it was virtuous. It described the power of their mythical gods when they performed a heroic deed.

In many ways, virtue is the life-quality that places its stamp of approval on all these other character qualities of life. To fail at being virtuous is to fail at everything else. You can be talented, knowledgeable, capable, gifted, and have other remarkable abilities . . . however, if you are not believed to be a person of virtue, you will not be trusted. Eventually you will fail in whatever life endeavor you are engaged.

Cleverness and brilliance can take you a long way in public life, for a time, but in the long run it fails miserably unless that brilliance is matched by virtue.

In the broadest biblical sense, "virtue" means: "intrinsic eminence, moral goodness, moral character, and reliability." Virtue is a high state of moral ability perfected over the years by walking consistently with God. Virtue is that condition, whereby, any day, any weekend, we can be sure that the person of virtue is living a righteous life, no matter what pressures may be placed on them or what temptations are placed before them.

Vice has become pandemic in our day. This generation, for want of virtue, is not only sinning and sinful, but it's also shameless. Our society is progressing like the poet Alexander Pope predicted:

> Vice is a monster of so frightful mien,
> As to be hated needs but to be seen;
> Yet seen too oft, familiar with her face,
> We first endure, then pity, then embrace!

Dr. Paul Cameron and colleagues conducted research on 6,714 obituaries from 16 U.S. homosexual journals from 1981 through 1993, as compared to a large sample of obituaries from regular newspapers. The sampling from newspapers matched the U.S. averages for longevity. The median age of death of married men was 75; 80 percent of whom died at age 65 or older. The median age of death of unmarried or divorced men was 57; 32 percent of whom died at age 65 or older. The median age of death of married women was 79; 85 percent of whom died at age 65 or older. The median age of death of unmarried or divorced women was 71; 60 percent of whom had died at age 65 or older.

But the comparison of these statistics to the homosexual population is startling! Less than 2 percent of homosexuals survived to age 65! For homosexuals with AIDS, the median age of death was 39! For those whose death was from factors other than AIDS, it was 42! The survey also found that of the lesbians studied, the median age of death was 45! Only 23 percent survived to the age of 65 or older. Other factors about the homosexual community are also alarming . . . homosexuals are 116 times more likely to be murdered and 24 times more likely to commit suicide! There is no doubt that the homosexual lifestyle is a very dangerous one, according to Dr. Paul Cameron and his study.

Nearly every critical issue of our society today is connected to a problem of morality! In our time we have seen statesmanship become politics, music become noise, enthusiasm become cynicism, love become sex, immorality become preference, and sin become choice. It's become so bad that some of the cynical, liberal leaders are now calling for the return of moral principles into our society.

Never has there been a day when virtue was more desperately needed. We need to live out in real life the divine qualities and character traits that make us more like Jesus Christ. What an opportunity.

GOODNESS AS EXCELLENCE: When used in this context, goodness as excellence is used to denote the proper fulfillment of anything. What is the excellence of a person? There's a hint contained in Peter's writings, "His divine power has given us everything we need for life and godliness through our knowledge of Him who called us by His own glory and GOODNESS" (2 Pet. 1:3). Here he uses it as speaking of the impact of Christ's character on any person, which in turn will lead that person to making a commitment to a particular lifestyle. Here he makes the claim that the same quality of life that is a quality of God can also be worked out in the character and living of each and every believer.

In a word, then, our living must reflect something of the very attractive character of the person of Jesus Christ. He was the person, par excellence, the model, the example. We're talking about living out in practical goodness as virtue and excellence.

Julie A. Manhan has written the following: There was once a little boy who wanted to meet God. He knew it was a long trip to where God lived, so he packed his suitcase with Twinkies and a six-pack of root beer and he started his journey.

When he had gone about three blocks, he met an old woman. She was sitting in the park just staring at some pigeons. The boy sat down next to her and opened his suitcase. He was about to take a drink from his root beer when he noticed that the old lady looked hungry, so he offered her a Twinkie. She gratefully accepted it and smiled at him. Her smile was so pretty that the boy wanted to see it again, so he offered her a root beer. Once again she smiled at him. The boy was delighted!

They sat there all afternoon eating and smiling, and never said a word. As it grew dark, the boy realized how tired he was and he got up to leave, but before he had gone more than a few steps, he turned around, ran back to the old woman, and gave her a hug. She gave him her biggest smile ever.

When the boy opened the door to his own house a short time later, his mother was surprised by the look of joy on his face. She asked him, "What did you do today that made you so happy?"

He replied, "I had lunch with God." But before his mother could respond, he added, "You know what? She's got the most beautiful smile I've ever seen!"

Meanwhile, the old woman, also radiant with joy, returned to her home. Her son was stunned by the look of peace on her face and asked, "Mother, what did you do today that made you so happy?"

She replied, "I ate Twinkies in the park with God." But before her son responded, she added, "You know, he's much younger than I expected."

Make every effort to add to your life . . . GOODNESS!

TODAY'S BIBLE READING: I Peter 4:1-19

37.
WHAT IS REAL?

We live in a world where it's getting harder to tell the real from the make believe. As this new development, "virtual reality," comes more and more into use, the lines between the real and the faux are more and more blurred. "What is real?" is one of those ultimate kinds of questions much like "What is truth?" Is it real if it can be identified with one of our five senses?

Within each person there is a longing for something real, something lasting, something that can be counted on. This is part of the eternal searching that seems to be such a vital part of the growing up process. It can become most acute during those teen years which are so vital, sometimes it begins in adolescence. Such times call for the very best from mothers to be understanding, to be loving, to be forgiving, to be a guide, to be a mentor, or just to be a quiet listener as a child struggles with the concept. This searching and seeking for the real can take some people down lots of dead-end searches before they find themselves. It can be a frustrating search.

It's relatively easy to discover that birth, life, and death are real. And this world has a way of confronting all of us with the reality of what life is all about. But in this search, at some point, there must be the discovery of something real that transcends this material world. It's a search for the eternal, it's an attempt to fill the God-shaped vacuum inside each person. It's a moment when mortality is confronted with the eternal. For what and for whom shall my life be patterned? Jesus Christ, the only Person who has been a resident of heaven first, then earth, challenged all of us with the real, "I am the way, the truth, and the life!" There it is. Believe it or refuse it. There is really no neutral ground.

 This being a mentor during this discovery stage can be vastly shortened if you, personally, have discovered what is real in your life. Everything of this earth will someday pass away. It's in transition. And with the acceleration of information and virtual reality increasing, it is imperative that you are secure in this discovery and that you can guide somebody else to make the same choices. You might enjoy the following short excerpt from a wonderful children's book, *The Velveteen Rabbit*, which deals with our subject:

The Skin Horse had lived longer in the nursery than any of the others. He was so old that his brown coat was bald in patches and showed the seams underneath, and most of the hairs in his tail had been pulled out to string bead necklaces. He was wise, for he had seen a long succession of mechanical toys arrive to boast and swagger, and by-and-by break their mainsprings and pass away, and he knew that they were only toys. For nursery magic is very strange and wonderful, and only those playthings that are old, wise, and experienced like the Skin Horse understand all about it.

"What is Real?" asked the Rabbit one day, when they were lying side by side near the nursery fender, before Nana came to tidy the room. "Does it mean having things that buzz inside you and a stick-out handle?"

"Real isn't how you are made," said the Skin Horse. "It's a thing that happens to you. When a child loves you for a long, long time, not just to play with, but REALLY loves you, then you become REAL."

"Does it hurt?" asked the Rabbit.

"Sometimes," said the Skin Horse. "When you are Real you don't mind being hurt."

"Does it happen all at once, like being wound up," he asked, "or bit by bit?"

"It doesn't happen all at once," said the Skin Horse. "You become. It takes a long time. That's why it doesn't often happen to people who break easily, or have sharp edges, or who have to be carefully kept. Generally, by the time you are Real, most of your hair has been loved off, and your eyes drop out and you get loose in the joints and very shabby. But these things don't matter at all, because once you are Real you can't be ugly."

TODAY'S BIBLE READING: John 8:12-59

38.
HOW COURAGE IS TAUGHT

Courage is one of those characteristics every mother hopes is instilled in each of her children. But how? Let's first start with what it is. According to Random House College Dictionary, "courage" is "the quality of mind or spirit that enables a person to face difficulty, danger, pain, etc., with firmness and without fear; bravery."

There are many facets to this life quality . . . it's like holding up a cut stone to the light and seeing the facets, but it is still the same stone. Courage can take many forms . . . bravery, valor, fearlessness, dauntlessness, stout-heartedness, intrepidity, daring, boldness, nerve, derring-do, fortitude, guts, pluck, spunk, mettle, grit, indomitable, stalwart, and even heroism. And I trust that you will agree with me that such qualities of mind and spirit need to be put into the soul of every person. But how? I have a deep impression that courage is not easily taught . . . it's something that goes beyond the classroom. In order for it to be copied it must first be seen. Before a younger one can live it out it must be observed in the lifestyle of a mentor. It's easier to demonstrate than it is to talk about. Seeing it in action speaks louder than any words used to encourage it.

Let this real life story as told by William Jones of Oklahoma City give us a clue on teaching courage:

Her name was Adelia and the lessons of courage that she taught are unsurpassed in my life. But how does one "teach" courage? Permit me to share her teachings.

Adelia's oldest son (we will call him Will) was exceptionally bright. At the age of 12, however, and before the age of antibiotics, Will was stricken with a series of infections that destroyed most of his ability to function mentally as a normal person. From that age until his death at 56, his mother entirely cared for his needs. She slaved, fed, bathed, dressed, and attended to his restroom needs for 44 years. The half-dozen words he could say were understood by her alone.

Adelia protected her son from those "making fun of him," mostly grandsons. The truth is that we were afraid of him because of his strange ways, like "Boo" in "To Kill a Mockingbird."

Other members of the family tried in vain to get Adelia to put Will in a rest home (known as the "county farm" in those days). They felt she was wasting her life and needed some time of her own. On one occasion, insistent family members prevailed upon her to try the new arrangement. At the end of the first week, both Adelia and Will were stressed beyond belief. The family brought him home and peace was restored to both lives.

When will reached the age of 56 he became desperately ill. But while Will was ill in one room, his father (we will call him Robert) was terminally ill in another room. On a winter day in 1949 both men died, Will in the morning and Robert that afternoon. She was overwhelmed with grief, but the greater loss seemed to surround the son she had nursed for 44 years. Soon a double funeral was held (the only one I have ever known not resulting from an accident). Two years later she found her resting place between Will and Robert.

You might have felt that now Adelia could make a life for herself since her burdensome responsibility had ended. But she never seemed to find life again. Did her life end in tragedy? Many would say yes, the waste of a beautiful life that could have been devoted to her other four children and her grandchildren. Such persons would have suggested she "take a walk" and leave the whole tragic scene behind.

But her teachings were most profound in her devotion to a helpless son, a true lesson of courage, and one that none of us ever forgot. Since Adelia's death, two of her children have had similar experiences in their families. In addition, one grandson has been faced with a similar responsibility. Not one of these has failed to meet their responsibilities, including this grandson. With the "teaching" of courage in Adelia's life, would the results have been the same? Only God knows for sure, but I will give her the credit all my days.[15]

Courage is better caught than taught!

TODAY'S BIBLE READING: Esther 4:1-17

39.
MOTHERS WHO LAUGH…LAUGH WITH GOD

Somewhere between childhood innocence and now, life has become much too grim. When did a well-exercised sense of humor and joy get sacrificed on the altar of adulthood? Who says that being a Christian means having a long face? Who? Too many people all of us know look like they are holding down a night job at the local mortuary.

Speaking about morticians, as a pastor I've had the privilege of meeting many of them and some of them have a well-developed sense of humor in order to survive. Mike was one of my favorites. He'd called on me to conduct a funeral for a woman who had died in a fire. This woman was not a church member, so Mike called me to do the honors. We're walking down the hall, alongside of the chapel towards the front when he stops, listens, turns to me and starts laughing uproariously, "Listen," he gasps, "Mary [the chapel organist] is playing, 'Smoke Gets in Your Eyes'!" We have a good laugh and it's time for the funeral to begin and I need to appear properly somber and cleric-like. Oh, well. . . .

Do you need strength for your day? Find help in joy! Do you need help — the answer is in finding joy. Do you want to express the fruit of the Spirit — do it joyfully! Do you celebrate the goodness of God — do it with joy! Are you hurting and need to recover — recovery is in being joyful!

For the Christian, laughter and joyfulness are first attitudes, then actions. Attitudes are formed by convictions. Therefore, Christians have developed strong convictions as to who they are, where they are going, who God is, what His love is all about, know His Word, and have learned to experience joy. I like the way Chuck Swindoll says it, "Laughter is a joy flowing, happiness showing, countenance glowing, kind of attitude."

I'll just throw this in . . . as a pastor, making observations of many people over a number of years, I have never seen anyone become lukewarm or go back on the life commitment if they have kept alive the joy of their salvation.

Now here's a test: How pastoral are you? Would you like to be a pastor? How would you have handled the following pastoral test?

A female pastor, who shall remain unnamed, had recently been installed as a new pastor in a medium-size town to pastor a medium-size church. It's Saturday night, and she has two worship services to prepare for the next morning, along with family responsibilities. The phone awakens her about midnight, she picks up the receiver and hears the obvious sounds of a party going full swing in the background. A voice says, "Pastor, since you are new to this town, and a recent graduate from seminary, we are having a discussion, and you can settle our dispute. What was Lot's wife's name?" Now what would you do?

This pastor wrote down their phone number and promised to call back. She looked up the answer, set the alarm to go off at 4:00 a.m. and went back to bed. At four, she called them — and boy, oh boy, did they ever sound sleepy — and answered, "Lot's wife is not named in the Bible."

Now that may not have been the most loving thing to do . . . but in her own words, "It sure felt good at the time!"

Can you imagine serving a God that laughs? Here's some information from Psalm 2:4, "The One enthroned in heaven laughs!" Jesus Christ, God's only begotten Son, was not dressed in black clothing or sackcloth and ashes! While He was among us on earth . . . He was worshiped by women and loved by little kids. Women and kids are not attracted to somber, sober, kill-joy types of men. Here's what God says about this special Son: "About the Son he says . . . your God, has set you above your companions by anointing you with the oil of joy" (Heb. 1:9).

In the Gospel accounts, Jesus is pictured as a warm friend, full of life, given to laughter, sharing good news to all, and a great party guest! NOW — let's just start working on those 150 laughs per day!

TODAY'S BIBLE READING: Hebrews 1:1-14

40.
STRENGTH COMES FROM JOY

The Reverend Oscar Johnson, jovial St. Louis clergyman, tells this story on himself: Once after a change of churches, I met a woman of my former flock and asked, "How do you like your new pastor?"

"Just fine," she beamed, "but somehow or other, he just doesn't seem to hold me like you did."

In order to become a survivor in life . . . learn how to be joyful and full of laughter. And from the biblical point of view, being joyful is just good medicine. I remind you that one of the wisest men to ever live wrote it first, "A cheerful heart is good medicine" (Prov. 17:22). If it's good medicine . . . it should have benefits that are psychological, cardiovascular, and muscular.

This leads us to the magnificent letter written to the people who lived in Philippi, Paul's letter to the Philippian Church. It has only 104 verses. As it's read, even today, it brings a smile. As we read along we discover that this church which he had had a hand in founding about ten years previously, holds some wonderful memories of people. Not only that, but as we look over his shoulder as he pens these happy words from a Roman prison, we can discover his secret of joy which can be our secret of joy. Here's a person who learned how to live joyfully in spite of his circumstances. How?

JOY COMES FROM HAPPY MEMORIES! Joy floods the mind of Paul when he recalls the happy memories of the people who were a part of that church. You can read about it from the first chapter in this letter to the Philippians.

He was much like Pastor William Goodin, who recalls: "One of the wildest, most fun-loving congregations I had the privilege of serving was a small church in Washington state. During our ministry there, they had an ugly baby contest; a General George Custer memorial ice cream feed on the date Custer was creamed at Little Big Horn; a Joan of Arc memorial barbecue on the date Joan was burned at the stake; a party door prize that was a door; piñatas filled with peanut butter, and you can't imagine the mess of that one; and musical onion, where the potent veggie is passed around and then eaten when the music stops. After seven great years with that wild bunch, I started fearing that I would not know how to minister to 'normal' people."

Paul wrote, "I always pray with joy because of your partnership in the gospel" (Phil. 1:4-5). His memory of them made him smile. What a way to remember and recall others. What a way to live . . . no regrets, no nursed bitter feelings, no unresolved conflicts . . . just happy memories! Therefore it is important that we work on the present so the memories of today will also be joyful.

One more from Pastor Goodin as he recalls a most memorable ice cream social and cake auction at their church. At one point the bidding for a cake was up to $26 and going hot and heavy. The chief bidder finally asked, "WHO is bidding against me?"

The auctioneer answered, "Nobody, why?"

At the same event the year previous, a beautiful cherry-covered cheese cake was going for $15. From the back of the room a voice called out, "I'll give you $30 for it if you will put it in Paul's face." (Paul was chairman of the board.) The auctioneer looked around, saw Paul behind him not paying attention, and quickly said, "$30! Going, going . . . WHAP . . . gone!" And there stood our esteemed chairman, looking rather surprised and very nicely covered with cherries and cheese cake.

Such fond memories of people. Paul must have had some of those as he spoke of the confidence in God who was still at work in their lives, "He who began a good work in you will carry it on to completion until the day of Christ Jesus" (Phil. 1:6).

Don't forget this principle: Joy comes from happy memories of people!

JOY COMES FROM A MIND THAT IS FOCUSED! Why has the joyful life-attitude been so elusive for so many Christians? Most people think that happiness and joyfulness is something that happens to them rather than something to be deliberately chosen. Yes, there are all kinds of things which can rob us of our joy . . . but joy comes to those who determine to chase after joy in all kinds of circumstances, regardless. Choose right!

If you are waiting for the circumstances to get just right so that you can be joyful, you will never be joyful again! It's not a gift delivered to your door by UPS every morning, it's a choice!

JOY CAN BE REPRODUCED IN ALL OF US AS WE USE THE SECRET INGREDIENT: ACTION! Yes, I know, life can be complicated and full of dilemmas and choices that may not be real choices. Somehow, most of us seem to end up with more gray choices that those black or white, clear-cut choices.

We can identify with poor ole Charlie Brown. It seems that in one episode Lucy is philosophizing and Charlie is listening. She has the floor and is delivering one of her dogmatic lectures. "Charlie Brown," she begins, "life is a lot like a deck chair. Some place it so they can see where they're going. Others place it to see where they've been. And some so they can see where they are at the present."

Charlie sighs and says, "I can't even get mine unfolded."

The key to making all of this joyfulness work for us comes alive, "Whatever happens, *CONDUCT* [caps and italics are mine] yourselves in a manner worthy of the gospel" (Phil. 1:27). Conduct is behavior, ways, manner, action, deeds, direction, management, control, to carry on, to carry out, operate, execute, or follow. In plain English so all of us can understand, "Whatever happens, choose and do. . . ."

The Early Church practiced this living in joy, for example: In the days of the Early Church , the first church, the beginnings of Christianity, one heathen scoffer inquired in sarcasm, "What is your Carpenter doing now?"

And the answer of the unperturbed Christian was bold and expressed with a smile, "Making a coffin for your Emperor."

Joy is your choice which is helped along with happy memories of people and then produced by the secret ingredient of putting it into practice. *Conduct!* Joy is a choice!

TODAY'S BIBLE READING: Philippians 1:1-30

On Mother's Day all over the country, grateful moms are pushed back into their pillows, the flower on their bird-of-paradise plant (which blooms every other year for 15 minutes) is snipped and put in a shot glass, and a strange assortment of food comes out of a kitchen destined to take the sight from a good eye.

A mixer whirs, out of control, then stops abruptly as a voice cries, "I'm telling!"

A dog barks and another voice says, "Get his paws out of there. Mom has to eat that!"

Minutes pass and finally, "Dad! Where's the chili sauce?"

Then, "Don't you dare bleed on Mom's breakfast!"

The rest is a blur of banging doors, running water, rapid footsteps, and a high pitched, "YOU started the fire! YOU put it out!"

The breakfast is fairly standard: a water tumbler of juice, five pieces of black bacon that snap in half when you breathe on them, a mound of eggs that would feed a Marine division, and four pieces of cold toast.

The kids line up by the bed to watch you eat and from time to time ask why you're not drinking your Koolaid or touching the cantaloupe with black olives on top spelling "M-O-M."

Later in the day, after you have decided it's easier to move to a new house than clean the kitchen, you return to your bed where, if you're wise, you'll reflect on this day. For the first time, your children have given instead of received. They have offered up to you the sincerest form of flattery: trying to emulate what YOU do for THEM. And they have presented you with the greatest gift people can give: THEMSELVES.

There will be other Mother's Days and other gifts that will astound and amaze you. But not one of them will ever measure up to the sound of your children in the kitchen on Mother's Day whispering, "Don't you dare bleed on Mom's breakfast!"[16]

While we are on the subject of mothers and Mother's Day, let's take it a bit further. Here is a small collection of notes which have been written to Mother's with great affection on their special day from their kids. Enjoy. . . .

Dear Mother: I am going to make dinner for you for Mother's Day. It's going to be a surprise. Your daughter, Angie H., age 8 (Seattle) P.S.: I hope you like pizza and popcorn.

Dear Mother: I got you a turtle for Mother's Day. I hope you like the turtle I got you this year for Mother's Day better than the snake I got you for Mother's Day last year. Your son, Robert H., age 8 (Portland, Maine)

Dear Mother: I wish Mother's Day wasn't always on Sunday. It would be better if it was on Monday so we wouldn't have to go to school. Love, Aileen W., age 9 (Baltimore)

Dear Mother: I hope you like the flowers I got you for Mother's Day. I picked them myself when Mr. Smith wasn't looking. Your daughter, Diane P., age 8 (Cincinnati)

Dear Mom: Arthur and I promise not to fight all day for Mother's Day. Your son, Billy G., age 9 (Dallas)

Dear Mother: Here is the box of candy I bought you for Mother's Day. It is very good candy because I already ate three of the pieces. Love, Marcy C., age 8 (Washington, DC)

Dear Mother: Here are two aspirins. Have a happy Mother's Day. Love, Carole H., age 8 (Los Angeles)

Tony Compolo writes: Too many times women are made to feel that they should apologize for being mothers and housewives. In reality, such roles can be noble callings. When I was on the faculty of the University of Pennsylvania, there were gatherings from time to time to which faculty members brought their spouses. Inevitably, some woman lawyer or sociologist would confront my wife with the question, "And what is it that you do, my dear?"

My wife who is one of the most brilliantly articulate individuals I know, had a great response: "I am socializing two Homo Sapiens in the dominant values of the Judeo-Christian tradition in order that they might be instruments for the transformation of the social order into the teleologically prescribed utopia inherent in the eschaton."

When she followed that with, "And what is it that you do?" the other person's, "A lawyer," just wasn't that over-powering.[17]

So, Mom, enjoy motherhood! Build great memories! Cherish those times with your kids because it won't last forever. What you do will be life-changing for some little person or persons!

TODAY'S BIBLE READING: Proverbs 14:1-35

42.
SOME SELECTED POETRY FOR MOTHERS

Next to the Bible, perhaps poetry has helped people more than any other kind of literary expression. Poetry has been used to bring conclusions to messages; has comforted people who are bereaved; has helped cheer the lonely; has brought hope where there is no hope; and encouraged the discouraged. Really, there is no limit to the power of anointed Christian poetry. It's my prayer that this little collection of poems will bless, encourage, and fill you with hope. Enjoy.

AT MY MOTHER'S KNEE

I have worshiped in churches and chapels,
I have prayed in the busy street;
I have sought my God and found Him
Where the waves of the ocean beat.
I have knelt in the silent forest,
In the shade of some ancient tree,
But the dearest of all my altars
Was raised at my mother's knee.

I have listened to God in His temple
I have caught His voice in the crowd;
I have heard Him speak when the breakers
Were booming long and loud;
When the winds play soft in the treetops,
My Father has talked to me;
But I never have heard Him clearer
Than I did at my mother's knee.

The things in my life that are worthy were born in my mother's breast;
And breathed into mine by the magic of the love her life expressed.
The years that have brought me to manhood have taken her far from me;
But memory keeps me from straying too far from my mother's knee.

God make me the man of her vision, and purge me of all selfishness!
God, keep me true to her standards, and help me to live to bless!
God, hallow the holy impress of the day that used to be,
And keep me a pilgrim forever to the shrine at my mother's knee.

(Croft M. Pentz)

MY MOTHER'S LOVE

Her love is like an island
In life's ocean, vast and wide,
A peaceful, quiet shelter
From the wind, the rain, the tide,

'Tis bound on the North by hope
By patience on the West,
By tender Counsel on the South
And on the East by rest.

Above it like a beacon light shine faith and truth and prayer;
And through the changing scenes of life I find a haven there.

(Croft M. Pentz)

GOD'S IDEAL MOTHER

The mother who owns Christ as Lord and Saviour in her life;
The mother who has peace with God, who has no inner strife;
The mother who knows how to trust the Father for all things;
The mother who is right and just, as punishment she brings.
The mother who knows how to pray for every daily need;
The mother who can point the way, where God would have her lead;
The mother who knows how to guide a precious child to God;
The mother who walks by His side, who walks the way He trod.

The mother who knows how to teach her child the Holy Word;
The mother who knows how to reach a child who has not heard;
The mother who knows how to show a loving, tender face;
The mother who can help him grow in wisdom and in grace.
The mother who can make a home, in any place on earth;
The mother, who, though children roam, has love that knows no dearth;
The mother who is all of this, to whom her God is real;
The mother who is not remiss, she is her God's ideal.

(Cora M. Pinkham)

HAPPINESS,

It's not so much the things without, the things you may possess
As money, riches, houses, land, that make for happiness;
Although the world may think so and seeks to thus attain,
Or strives for other outward things . . . at last we find them in vain.
A mind that's filled with noble thoughts, a heart that's fixed on God;
A will to do the honest things and walk where Jesus trod;
A purpose great, an aim that's high, a soul that's clear of sin . . .
This brings a happiness so sweet, and springs up from within![18]

(Walter Isenhour)

TODAY'S BIBLE READING: Psalm 119:1-48

43.
THE "X-FACTOR"
IN LIFE

The last two times my wife and I have stayed at one of the premier lakeside resorts in the Ozarks (which shall remain unidentified), there was no way you could wash your head with the hand-held shower because of the scalding water. It was on our annual staff retreat, during the off season, in which we were guests in the "Governor's Suite" no less. The previous year, when you turned on the shower, whether hot or cold controls, out poured steaming, scalding hot water . . . even with the cold on full blast! The following year, it still malfunctioned!

Here we were in one of the best accommodations the Ozarks has to offer and all we could get was a miserable hand-held shower that didn't work!

From our view from the top floor we could look out over beautiful Lake Taneycomo, one very exciting view, a view to kill for. The steam was rising over the lake as the sun was rising, gorgeous! The suite was really beautifully decorated, tastefully done in rustic. Everything worked except the shower/tub arrangements.

There, as we experienced it, the "X-Factor" strikes again! The X-Factor is everywhere! It's impossible to escape it as long as we are all part of the oh-sooo-human-race.

You've carefully planned for it . . . that wonderful once-in-a-lifetime getaway vacation. You have arrived, you're away from it all, no phones, all set for the most relaxing night's sleep in a long time. All your cares have been washed away on your flight to freedom. You turn the light off, just as you begin to doze off . . . you hear it! You cringe as you await the inevitable attack, the sound grows louder then fades, you hope it's gone, no, you know it's gone. Then, it's right by your ear, you feel it on your cheek, you slap your face, you missed, the buzzing goes away, you're wide awake! You turn the light on, you reach for a folded newspaper and set out in hot pursuit of the mosquito, you can't find it anywhere, it's disappeared . . . until you turn out the light and attempt to find that elusive sleep once more. The X-Factor in the form of a mosquito strikes again! Incidentally, did you know that only the female of the mosquito species bites?

It can happen anywhere at anytime. You've just driven that brand-new car off the dealer's lot, enjoying the thrill of the new-car smell. Then you remember that you must pick up a few items at the grocery store. You carefully park it away from other cars . . . only to return to discover that a rust-bucket of a pickup is next to your beauty on your return. Upon careful examination, there is a door-ding! It strikes again!

You're on vacation, staying in a condo in the gorgeous Vail valley in Colorado. Because of the clear, clean mountain air, you've left your window open. No cares . . . only the possibility of sleeping late in the morning. At about 6:00 a.m. the X-Factor makes an invasion into your quiet, decorator touched bedroom . . . "pocketa, pocketa, pocketa, POCKETA, POCKETA. . . . " You jump out of bed, what's going on? The sound has disappeared . . . only to gradually return! You're looking like crazy only to discover some maniac making passes outside your resort window in an ultra-light-plane! It strikes at home, too!

It's Christmas Eve, the family has all gathered for the festivities . . . it begins to snow, lightly, gently, softly . . . it's gorgeous. But as you busy yourself with the special Christmas Eve dinner, you fail to notice. The snowing is harder, now wet, heavy snow loading up all the trees, limbs begin to bend beneath the weight, that one tree in the backyard which should have been trimmed last summer is loading with the heavy wet stuff . . . then it snaps, falling on the power line from the pole in the alley. Everything goes black! Dark! No more electricity! The roast is ruined. Oh, well . . . ah, the X-Factor!

The thing about it, the X-Factor doesn't respect anybody's age, either. Childhood really has it. On the first day of summer vacation some hapless child breaks her arm! New shoes that wear a blister on the heel. Chicken pox over the Christmas holiday. A brand new bicycle that gets a scratch in the first tumble.

The teenage years are no better . . . it's the first really big date, and there's a huge pimple in the middle of your forehead!

It happens at all ages . . . even in retirement. You have saved and scrimped and saved and sacri-ficed and planned and saved some more to purchase that special motorhome so you can travel together and really do something you have always wanted to do, but couldn't — travel these United States . . . but your husband, on the first day from home is struck down by a heart attack! The X-Factor is merciless.

Why call this the "X-Factor"? What is it?

In what should be the happiest of all life-experiences, we are aware of the X-Factor! Life begins with it . . . out of the warm, comfortable, cozy, protected mother's womb into the cold, cruel, wide world . . . and SMACK!

Why? Do you ever think about it?

I've thought about it quite often . . . in fender dings, dislocated fingers, financial reversals, in emergency rooms waiting for stitches to be applied, standing in miserable showers, doing a pratfall on the platform.

For starters, this tinge of vileness keeps us from becoming too content with this earth becoming our eternal abode . . . with this earth as being our heaven. Someplace, not here, there must be rooms without mosquitoes, rooms with working showers, faces without pimples, arms that aren't broken at the most inopportune times, eyes that see more and more rather than less and less. It's to keep us from becoming too comfortable down here.

From the life of Abraham we can draw an interesting parallel to our day. As you read of his life, you discover that he was a pilgrim and he considered himself to be just a pilgrim passing through this life. And as such he "pitched" his tent and "built" his altars. But we in our sophistication of living have "pitched" our altars and "built" our tents. The X-Factor keeps us from getting too comfortable with our lifestyles.

Maybe this un-ending search we do looking for greener pastures is a leftover from the perfection which was created in the Garden of Eden. The X-Factor may also remind us of what things would have been like if mankind, meaning Adam and Eve and me and perhaps you, hadn't loused up this world with our sin problems.

Well to milk a bit more out of our subject at hand . . . the X-Factor also makes life most interesting and most challenging. Is it just possible that I, we, can learn to enjoy the view in spite of a lousy shower? Can we still have fun on the Big Date with a pimple smack dab in our forehead? Will I still be able to enjoy the meal when a child clumsily spills a glass of iced tea over the white tablecloth? Is it possible to whistle while bailing out a flooded basement; changing a flat tire on a cold, cold morning; stalking the invading mosquito; be happy even if the new car door collects the first ding? Yes or no?

Well, at least we try! Right? Right! I'm giving it my best shot. How about you? Ready to live in spite of the X-Factors or because of the X-Factors?

Paul the Apostle, now an old man, writes some words that may or may not be of comfort to you. "I am not saying this because I am in need, for I have learned to be content whatever the circumstances. I know what it is to be in need, and I know what it is to have plenty. I have learned the secret of being content in any and every situation . . . I CAN DO EVERYTHING THROUGH HIM WHO GIVES ME STRENGTH" (Phil. 4:11-13)!

Maybe . . . just maybe, we can learn, too!

TODAY'S BIBLE READING: Philippians 4:1-23

44.
HONEST WORSHIPING AND HYMN SINGING?

I can still remember it quite vividly . . . in the church in mid-central Minnesota where much of my growing up days were spent, occasionally there was a time when a children's choir formed and practiced to sing for the "big" people in a service. The song I most clearly remember (now you must know that we were six, seven, and eight years old) singing went like this: "Years I spent in vanity and pride/Caring not my Lord was crucified. . . ."

Now, we didn't deliberately set out to sing something that wasn't remotely true . . . our adult director made this unhappy choice for us. Back then, it didn't seem that too many caught it, but in retrospect, it was sure phony singing.

There were many more which have slipped from memory, but there was one more that seems a bit troubling: "I'll love Thee in life/I will love Thee in death. . . . " Now what does a seven year old really know about death? There was another favorite of our director: "My soul in sad exile was out on life's sea, So burdened with sin and distress. . . ." Six, seven, and eight year-olds were singing this?

I think we need to be more truthful in our worship and in our singing. A really honest hymnbook or chorus sheet would revise some of the old familiar words to say what we might really mean as we sing.

How about some of the following for an example:

"Take my life and let it be . . . /Yes, Lord, let it be, let it be."

"Early in the morning my song shall rise to Thee/Oh Lord, not surely an early morning, how early is early . . . ?"

"Oh for a thousand tongues to sing, My great Redeemer's praise/One tongue is hardly any use, so my voice I'll not raise."

"Amazing grace, how the sweet the sound/That saved a wretch like you. . . ."

"We worship and adore You, falling down before You/Not on your life will I humble myself to that extent. . . ."

"I will enter your gates with Thanksgiving in my heart/Could you believe that it's a minor miracle that I'm even here. . . ."

"All to Jesus I surrender, All to Him I freely give/Not my paycheck, not my boat, not my car, not my hobby, not my bank account. . . ."

"O Jesus, I have promised To serve Thee to the end/Did I miss something here . . . ?"

"God be with you till we meet again! By His counsels guide, uphold you/I hope I never meet this turkey any more, not ever again. . . ."

"If Jesus goes with me, I'll go, Anywhere/Except to my next door neighbors. . . ."

"Shall I empty-handed be/When retirement I shall see. . . ."

"The church's one foundation/Is tax-deductible. . . ."

"The strife is o'er, the battle done/Our church has split and our side has won. . . ."

"I love to tell the story/Of things I see down here below. . . ."

"Peace! peace! wonderful peace, Coming down from the Father above/But just to make sure, the door is locked and I have a loaded gun within. . . ."

"Onward, Christian soldiers! Marching as to war/Not me, I my draft-card have burned. . . ."

"I'm rejoicing night and day, As I walk the pilgrim way/Talk about grim. . . ."

"My heavenly home is bright and fair, I feel like traveling on/Yes, yes, yes. . . ."

"Have thy affections been nailed to the cross/Right now they are fixed on that special person in my life."

"When all my labors and trials are o'er/I can hardly wait. . . ."

"Fairest Lord Jesus! Ruler of all nature/Just don't get too near me. . . ."

"All glory, laud, and honor/I'd like a little bit myself. . . ."

Honesty in worship and praise may be a bit harder to attain than we had previously thought.

Perhaps, this is a moment to make a decision not to sin with our singing. To sing only what can be done with honesty. Is that asking too much? Another thought . . . will we be held accountable for the things we have sung, even if written by a songwriter who knows nothing about us or our life situation?

Jesus talked with a woman at the well and out of that came a startling truth to His followers which challenges us today: "A time is coming and has now come when the true worshipers will worship the Father in spirit and truth, for they are the kind of worshipers the Father seeks. God is spirit, and His worshipers must worship in spirit and in truth" (John 4:23-24)!

So the next time you are singing your worship and your praise . . . do a quick mental check: Can I sing this without lying to the Lord to whom I am offering my praise and worship?

TODAY'S BIBLE READING: John 4:1-42

45.
BECAUSE...
GOD TOLD ME!

Have you ever had a tough time dealing with a particular person . . . because they have claimed a certain advantage? Whenever there's a question about what to do, when to do it, how to do it, or what to say, that person claims the high ground. Their answer goes something like this: "The Lord told me such and such. . . ." And the problem with such an answer is that it simply ends the matter. How can you argue with the Lord? How do you counter that? With a, "No, the Lord just told me this is so and so . . . ?" Hardly.

The troubling aspect of this kind of end-it-all authority is that in some parts of our world this is considered to be a mark of spirituality. Whatever that might be. The problem with such an exchange is that it works, too often.

Maxwell Anderson has written *Anne of a Thousand Days*, and in it there is an interesting exchange between Henry VIII and Anne Boleyn. Let's eavesdrop. . . .

HENRY: "What I do is God's will."

BOLEYN: "Now, if a man or monarch could be sure of that . . . "

HENRY: "I've worked it out in my mind. I pray to God. I tell you this first, Boleyn. God answers prayer. That's known. Every morning I get on my knees and pray that what I do may be God's will. I pray Him to direct me . . . that whatever comes to my mind . . . whatever notion floods my heart . . . shall be God's will . . . and I only His instrument. Wherever I turn, whatever I do . . . whether to reach for food, or thread my way among the coursed paths of the law, or interpret the Holy Word, or judge men innocent . . . or guilty . . . every morning I pray to Him on my knees nothing shall rise in my brain or heart but He has wished it first. And since He answers prayer, and since

He's given me such heavy power to act, power for good and evil, He must answer this. He does answer. I find such peace in this, that not one morning my whole life long shall I fail these devotions. . . ."

BOLEYN: "This is noble of you, of course, but your Majesty realizes that it might possibly be used as an excuse for. . . ."

HENRY: "For what?"

BOLEYN: "For doing as you please."[19]

Something to think about. Talk about spiritual arm-twisting. There is no higher authority that can be evoked. Are we sure that God has really spoken to us, if we use this tactic? How can you be sure it's not something simply out of your own brain?

There are other ways in which other forms of "spiritual" arm-twisting can take place. Christian parents tend to be given to the next abuse — deferring decision-making.

It works like this: The words used are, "You decide" and it's applied to all kinds of situations. These words can be spoken by someone who has already revealed how they feel about a certain situation, then humbly defers to the other for the final decision making.

It can happen like this: The teen comes home from school and let's say there is a movie in town to which they have been invited. Now the question, "So, Mom and Dad, can I go?"

There's a silence which is broken by Mom who says, "Well, son, your father and I have already talked this over and you know that this is not a good movie for you to go to but this is a decision we've decided that you'll have to make for yourself. You decide."

The teen comes back with, "So I decide. The next morning I tell them I'm going to the movie because one of my best friends invited me and I want to be with him. Then, there's a really, really long silence. And I think Mom is going to cry."

Then Dad jumps in with: "You're really going?"

"Sure thing," the teen answers, "You both told me to decide and I decided. I'm going to the movie."

Well, in looking back, the teen tells us, "You can imagine, life at home has been miserable since I made my decision. I finally figured it out. They really didn't want me to make that decision. They gave me a ballot like in a rigged election with only one way to vote implied in their thinking."

God is not in the arm-twisting business. He never forces us into a corner with only one way out. Therefore . . . why should we resort to such tactics? Eventually they will backfire and set fire to one or more of our relationships.

Yes, the Lord is always the final authority on any kind of an issue . . . but do you really have that answer? Some of life is in the groping for and working through of an issue. The Lord also gave us a brain and He also acknowledged that it is possible to use that brain in dealing with each other and with Him, "Come, now, let's reason together" says the Lord. His word is chock-full of life principles which give us answers in dealing with a particular situation. A better plan is to saturate yourself with the Word, "Study to show yourselves approved unto God a workman that needs not to be ashamed" when it comes to "rightly dividing the Word of God."

Of course, Jesus himself, when tempted, did say, "It is written. . . ." then followed it with the life principle. Apparently, somewhere in His past, his parents had been active in arming Him with a working knowledge of God's Word. Perhaps this training was strengthened by the local synagogue and ingrained into His thinking by the local rabbi.

This is not to say that the Lord cannot directly speak to you and to me. But be very careful when claiming that He has given you life direction that is to be applied just "because God told me. . . ." Let's refer to the written Word for our guidance. It's simply more reliable than what comes through our brain.

TODAY'S BIBLE READING: 2 Timothy 2:14-26; 2 Peter 1:12-21

46.
SECRETS FOR BUILDING STRONG FAMILIES

Americans have been duped again! We have been led to believe for more than the past decade that home life is deteriorating at an ever-increasing alarming rate. The government's National Center for Health Statistics released a report saying that in 1981 there had been 2.4 million new marriages and 1.4 million divorces! Presto . . . one in every two marriages is ending in divorce! DON'T YOU BELIEVE IT! This is another example of a statistical lie. They completely overlooked the number of already existing marriages!

"What was left out is that there were 54 million other marriages that are going on very nicely, thank you," so wrote the pollster, Louis Harris. Each year, ONLY TWO PERCENT (2 percent) of existing marriages will actually end in divorce, according to Harris!

"A number of academics made a sensational splash and the media got a lot of mileage out of it," said Harris. And "ever since then, an indelible message has been chorused in church pulpits, academic broadsides, and political prophecies of doom for the American family. Yet in reality, the American family is surviving under enormous pressure." Harris began questioning these statistics after polling 3,001 persons for a family survey. The study showed a "glowing picture of the American family."

Among the finds of this Harris poll were these: 85 percent of families have a happy marriage; 94 percent are highly satisfied with family relationships; 86 percent said they are happy with the support they receive from family members during a crisis, and only 20 percent said they are not happy with family life! Harris called the one-to-two divorce-marriage-ratio "one of the most specious pieces of statistical nonsense ever perpetrated in modern times."

Nick Stinnett, professor of Human Development and Family Life at the University of Alabama, and John DeFrain, associate professor in the department of Human Development and the Family at the University of Nebraska, have decided one of the reasons the media focus on the negative side of family life is they have no statistics on the positive side. They devised a program called the "Family Strengths Project."

They placed a notice in 48 newspapers in 25 different states which said: "If you live in a strong family, please contact us. We know a lot about what makes families fail; we need to know more about what makes them succeed." More than 3,000 letters poured in. When tabulated, out of that response, they discovered that six keys were mentioned time and time again. So what are these qualities?

1) COMMITMENT: This quality, according to Random House Dictionary is "to give in trust or charge or consign, the act of pledging, a promise to perform, to bind and to involve."

These committed people expected their families to last. In these homes, the family comes first. Here commitment and sexual fidelity are linked in such a strong way that any kind of an extramarital affair is viewed as an ultimate threat to the strength of the home.

2) TIME SPENT TOGETHER: In another survey, 1,500 children were asked: "What do you think makes a happy family?" As a group they didn't list any such things as money, cars, animals, games, recreation activities, or nice houses. Together they replied: "Doing things together." What to do doesn't seem to be as important as just doing it. Even working together is as effective as playing together or vacationing together. Just do it!

3) GIVING HONEST APPRECIATION: One mother in this survey wrote: "Each night we go into the children's bedrooms and give each a big hug and kiss. Then we say, 'You are really good kids and we love you very much.' We think it's important to leave that message with them at the end of the day."

To appreciate is to be grateful for, to value highly, to be fully aware of the value and to raise someone in value. What a beautiful thing to do for a family member. This is one of the most basic of human needs . . . to be appreciated.

4) DEVELOP GOOD COMMUNICATION: Here is the foundational bedrock principle of building any kind of lasting relationship. This doesn't happen when you get married or when you give birth to kids. It must be cultivated, it must be worked at, make it a major project. It's so easy to fail or to misunderstand.

A little girl came home from school and said to her mother, "I wish you would let me take a bath in the morning before I go to school instead of at night before I go to bed."

"What difference does it make?" her mother asked.

"Every day at school," the little girl said, "Miss Taylor tells everybody to stand up who had a bath today. And I haven't been able to stand up one time since school started three months ago."

5) COPING SUCCESSFULLY WITH ANY CRISIS: Even good, strong families have problems. The difference is that they have found a way to meet life challenges.

There are some simple things to remember when managing any crisis: Focus on the positive side, use those skills learned in communication, let that sense of humor be a buffer, be flexible, and learn how to call upon spiritual resources. Part of learning how to cope is to prepare ahead of time. Build in some safeguards.

6) DEVELOP A SPIRITUAL WELLNESS: To many people who were involved in making this survey, this was the most surprising of all the findings. "Spiritual wellness" was defined by strong families as a "caring center within each of us that promotes sharing, love, and compassion for others." It's much more than simply being a church-going family. It is a dimension of expressing in daily living what they were preaching and teaching.

It's a living out of biblical principles in real life. It's taking the Word of God and living it in the daily give-and-take of family life. Kids need to know about God, the concept of God, and they need to be introduced to God at an early age.

In the "Family Strengths Project" one lady wrote: "I put love into my family as an investment in their future, my future, our future. It's the best investment I can make!"[20]

A healthy, strong, caring, loving family is the place we enter for comfort, development, and regeneration. It's a place from which we can leave and be recharged for positive living!

And here's the very bottom line: "Unless the Lord builds the house, its builders labor in vain. Unless the Lord watches over the city, the watchmen stand guard in vain" (Ps. 127:1).

TODAY'S BIBLE READING:
Psalm 121:1-8; 127:1-5; 128:1-6

47.
MOTHERHOOD
...AND TOP PAY

The kids are fighting!

I have my hands over my ears again.

It's summer, hot . . . but fall is coming and winter is closing in.

I will spend the days ahead heating soup, dressing Aaron and Micah ten times over for sledding every day, reading Dr. Seuss before their too-short naps at noon.

My younger sister, unmarried, will be a vice president of a leasing company one day soon, my parents say. She spent a recent vacation in Mexico and last week's vacation at some very swank resort on the West Coast.

We spent our family vacation on a lake in a little rented cabin, Mark and I teaching the two boys to fish, catching toads, and crayfish. I made burgers, vacuumed sand, did laundry by hand.

Winter is coming, soon.

Oh, dear Lord, I want a job, a sweet, sweet check in hand, value spelled out in dollar signs to match my self-esteem, my pride. When someone asks what I do, I will know what I am paid, my worldly worth.

I want a job, I do.

I looked at the ads this morning, Lord, until Aaron, milky from breakfast, insisted himself into my lap, his heart between the pages.

"What are you doing, Mama? Do you love me? Read to me out of these pages, Mama. I love you."

A chubby hug.

How do I tell him: Get down. I want to read the employment ads. I want some other job that pays.

This one will not do. You children fight and play too loud and winter is coming soon and no, this will not do.

How do I tell him any of that as he sits in my lap?

I want a job, a job that pays.

How difficult some days to remember that there are other ways to measure self-esteem than a rectangular paper check. How easy to forget in the classified ads, how sweet to remember as I hug the child in my lap. I have a job, I do, and I am paid, not once a week with processed pulp, but every day.

"I love you Mama, I do."

Sometimes, in a world that measures everything in terms of hourly wage, the wealth of words gets very lost indeed. I love you is set on air, lands without a murmur on the heart.

The check is concrete in hand.

Values are torn apart.

I want a job that pays, Lord. What exactly do I do? How much do I make?

"I love you." Words from a small son's heart. Top pay!

I love you guys, too.[21]

TODAY'S BIBLE READING: Proverbs 31:1-31

48.
TEN COMMANDMENTS FOR PARENTS

Have you heard about the young man who wrote his first book? It was titled *Ten Commandments for Raising Kids*.

He later married and became a first-time father, revising his book and re-titling it to say *Ten Suggestions for Raising Kids*.

A bit later, another child arrived, then a third, and it was time to revise his book once more. This time, the new title became *Ten Hints for Raising Kids*.

After another one arrived and he became a first-time grandparent, the final revision of his book was made. The new title? *Ten Things I Don't Know about Raising Kids*.

Well . . . so much for the "commandment" type of advice. However, let's allow Dr. Kevin Leman to give us his version of the TEN COMMANDMENTS FOR PARENTS. Enjoy.

I. My hands are small; please don't expect perfection whenever I make a bed, draw a picture, or throw a ball. My legs are short; slow down so that I can keep up with you.

II. My eyes have not seen the world as yours have; let me explore it safely, don't restrict me unnecessarily.

III. Housework will always be there; I'm little only for a short time. Take time to explain things to me about this wonderful world, and do so willingly.

IV. My feelings are tender; don't nag me all day long (you would not want to be nagged for your inquisitive-ness). Treat me as you would like to be treated.

V. I am a special gift from God; treasure me as God intended you to do . . . holding me accountable for my actions, giving me guidelines to live by, and disciplining me in a loving manner.

VI. I need your encouragement (but not your empty praise) to grow. Go easy on the criticism; remember, you can criticize the things I do without criticizing me.

VII. Give me the freedom to make decisions concerning myself. Permit me to fail, so that I can learn from my mistakes. Then someday I'll be prepared to make the decisions life will require of me.

VIII. Don't do things over for me; that makes me feel that my efforts didn't measure up to your expectations. I know it's hard, but don't compare me with my brother or my sister.

IX. Don't be afraid to leave for a weekend together. Kids need vacations from parents, and parents need vacations from kids. Besides, it's a great way to show us kids that your marriage is something special.

X. Take me to Sunday school and church regularly, setting a good example for me to follow. I enjoy learning more about God.

Well said, Dr. Leman. Lots of truth and lots of common sense wisdom for raising kids in today's environment. He has reminded us all of things we already know about kids . . . but need the reminding once more.

Raising kids is something like holding a wet bar of soap . . . grasp it too firmly and it squirts away . . . but to get the most out of that soap, it needs water and a bit of scrubbing to make it effective. Raising good kids doesn't just happen. It's a responsibility, God-given, which demands the best from parents in order to be effective, nurturing, loving, caring, and patient parents. And it takes committed parents to make a home. The most important thing a father can do for his kids is to love their mother . . . the most important thing a mother can do for her kids is to love their father! And then, as parents, to love God!

TODAY'S BIBLE READING: Exodus 20:1-21

49.
THE GIFT

It was Sunday . . . Christmas. Our family had spent the holidays in San Francisco with my husband's parents. But in order for us to be back at work on Monday, we found ourselves driving the 400 miles back home to Los Angeles on Christmas day. We stopped for lunch in King City. The restaurant was nearly empty. We were the only family and ours were the only children.

I heard Erik, my one-year-old, squeal with glee: "Hithere." (Two words he thought were one.) "Hithere." He pounded his fat baby hands . . . whack, whack . . . on the metal high chair tray. His face was alive with excitement, eyes wide, gums bared in a toothless grin. He wriggled and chirped and giggled, and then I saw the source of his merriment . . . and my eyes could not take it all in at once.

A tattered rag of a coat . . . obviously bought by someone else, eons ago . . . dirty, greasy, and worn . . . baggy pants . . . spindly body . . . toes that poked out of would-be shoes . . . a shirt that had ring-around-the-collar all over, and a face like none other . . . gums as bare as Erik's. "Hi there baby; hi there, big boy. I see ya, buster."

My husband and I exchanged a look that was a cross between "What do we do?" and "poor devil."

Our meal came, and the cacophony continued. Now the old bum was shouting from across the room: "Do ya know patty cake? Atta boy . . . Do ya know peek-a-boo? Hey, look, he knows peek-a-boo!"

Erik continued to laugh and answer, "Hithere."

Every call was echoed. Nobody thought it was cute. The guy was a drunk and a disturbance. I was embarrassed. My husband, Dennis, was humiliated. Even our six year old said, "Why is that old man talking so loud?"

Dennis went to pay the check, imploring me to get Erik and meet him in the parking lot. "Lord, just let me out of here before he speaks to me or Erik." I bolted for the door.

It soon was obvious that both the Lord and Erik had other plans.

As I drew closer to the man, I turned my back, walking to sidestep him . . . and any air he might be breathing. As I did so, Erik, all the while with his eyes riveted to his best friend, leaned far over my arm, reaching with both arms to a baby's "pick-me-up" position.

In a split second of balancing my baby and turning to counter his weight I came eye-to-eye with the old man.

Erik was lunging for him, arms spread wide.

The bum's eyes both asked and implored, "Would you let me hold your baby?"

There was no need for me to answer since Erik propelled himself from my arms to the man's. Suddenly a very old man and a very young baby consummated their love relationship. Erik laid his tiny head upon the man's ragged shoulder. The man's eyes closed, and I saw tears hover beneath his lashes. His aged hands full of grime and pain and hard labor . . . gently, so gently, cradled my baby's bottom and stroked his back. I stood awestruck.

The old man rocked and cradled Erik in his arms for a moment, and then his eyes opened and set squarely on mine. He said in a firm commanding voice, "You take care of this baby."

Somehow I managed, "I will," from a throat that contained a stone.

He pried Erik from his chest . . . unwillingly, longingly . . . as though he was in pain.

I held my arms open to receive my baby and again the gentleman addressed me.

"God bless you, ma'am. You've given me my Christmas gift."

I said nothing more than a muttered thanks.

With Erik back in my arms, I ran for the car. Dennis wondered why I was crying and holding Erik so tightly and why I was saying, "My God, my God, forgive me."[22]

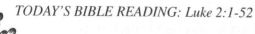 *TODAY'S BIBLE READING: Luke 2:1-52*

50.
THE LIGHT THAT SHINES IN A DARK PLACE

The society of the world in which we live is one of doubt, skepticism, cynicism, and unbelief. Into this darkness, biblical prophecy shines like "a light shining in a dark place, until the day dawns and the morning star arises in your hearts" (2 Pet. 1:19). Let's just consider one aspect of who and what Jesus Christ was all about.

Did you know that there are approximately 320 different, specific prophecies written in the Bible, before His birth, which were fulfilled during the 33 years of His life while here on earth. On the day of His crucifixion, 35 different, separate, and distinctive biblical prophecies were fulfilled. We can easily say that the biography of Christ was written centuries BEFORE He was born. Think of that impact . . . a life written about before birth and life!

Any time is a good time to think about and read again these biblical prophecies and how they were fulfilled.

	PROPHESIED	FULFILLED
1. He would be born in Bethlehem.	Micah 5:2	Matthew 2:1
2. He would be born of a virgin.	Isaiah 7:14	Luke 2:7
3. He would be called out of Egypt.	Hosea 11:1	Matthew 2:15
4. The children of Bethlehem would be slain.	Jeremiah 31:15	Matt. 2:16-18
5. He would teach in parables.	Psalm 78:2	Matthew 13:34-35
6. The mission statement of His public ministry.	Isaiah 61:1-2	Luke 4:16-21
7. He would be betrayed by a friend.	Psalm 41:9	John 13:18
8. The betrayal price of 30 pieces of silver.	Zechariah 11:12-13	Matthew 26.15

9. He would be rejected by the Jewish leaders.	Psalm 118:22	John 7:48
10. The nailing of hands and feet.	Psalm 22:16	John 19:18
11. The gall and vinegar He was given to drink.	Psalm 69:21	Matthew 27:34, 48
12. The soldiers would gamble for His garments.	Psalm 22:18	Matthew 27:35
13. None of His bones would be broken.	Psalm 34:20	John 19:36
14. He would be spat upon and scourged.	Isaiah 50:6	Mark 14:56
15. He would be forsaken of God.	Psalm 22:1	Matthew 27:46
16. He would be buried with the rich.	Isaiah 53:9	Matthew 27:57-60
17. His side would be pierced.	Zechariah 12:10	John 19:37
18. He would rise from the dead.	Psalm 68:18	Matthew 16:21
19. He would ascend to Heaven.	Psalm 16:10	Acts 1:9
20. He would establish an everlasting Kingdom.	Daniel 2:44	Hebrews 12:22-28 [23]

Now these are a listing of only 20 out of the more than 320 written, biblical prophecies! Is it just possible that the fulfillment of such prophecies could have happened by mere coincidence?

Think about this — Peter Stoner, in *Science Speaks,* calculates that the odds of any eight of these prophecies having been accidentally fulfilled in the life of one man would have been 1 in 100,000,000,000,000,000! Absolutely awesome . . . but such numbers are beyond most of us.

So suppose we would take 100,000,000,000,000,000 silver dollars and spread them all across the state of Texas. They would cover that state to a depth of about two feet. Then mark only one silver dollar with a red "X," which would have been scattered along with all the others. Then put a man or woman in an airplane, let them fly anywhere they want to over the state and then parachute to the ground which is covered in silver dollars. And upon landing, this person picks up the single silver dollar marked with the red "X." How likely is it that on the first try they might find the one with the red mark? Exactly the same kind of odds that the prophets had written just eight prophesies which would have been fulfilled hundreds of years later in the life of one person . . . JESUS CHRIST! [24]

In a large stone cathedral in Europe there was a large, magnificent pipe organ. It was a Saturday afternoon, and the sexton was making one final check of the choir and organ loft high in the balcony at the back of the church. He was startled to hear footsteps echoing up the stone stairway, as he thought the doors were all locked and no one was around. He turned to see a man in slightly tattered traveling clothes coming toward him. "Excuse me, sir," the stranger said. "I have come from quite a distance to see the great organ in this cathedral. Would you mind opening the console so that I might get a closer look at it?"

The custodian at first refused, but the stranger seemed so eager and insistent that he finally gave in. "May I sit on the bench?" That request of the stranger was met with absolute refusal by the custodian.

"What if the organist came in and found you sitting there? I would probably lose my job!" But again the stranger was so persistent that the sexton gave in. "But only for a moment," he added.

The custodian noticed that the stranger seemed to be very much at home on the organ bench, so he was not completely surprised when he was asked by the stranger to be allowed to play the organ. "No! Definitely not!" said the custodian. "No one is allowed to play it except the cathedral organist."

The man's face fell, and his deep disappointment was obvious. He reminded the custodian how far he had come and assured him that no damage would be done. Finally the sexton relented and told the stranger he could play the instrument, but only a few notes and then he would have to leave. Overjoyed, the stranger pulled out some stops and began to play. Suddenly the cathedral was filled with the most beautiful music the custodian had ever heard in all his years in that place. The music seemed to transport him heavenward.

In what seemed all too short a time, the dowdy stranger stopped playing and slid off the organ bench. And started down the stairway. "Wait!" cried the custodian. "That was the most beautiful music I have ever heard in the cathedral. Who are you?"

The stranger turned for just a moment as he replied, "Mendelssohn." The man was none other than Felix Mendelssohn, one of the greatest organists and composers of the 19th century!

The cathedral sexton was alone now in that great stone edifice, the beautiful organ music still ringing in his ears. "Just think," he said softly, "I almost kept the master from playing his music in my cathedral!"[25]

It's awesome to contemplate . . . that each one of us has the privilege of having a personal relationship with the Master of the universe, JESUS CHRIST! Let's not keep Him from playing His music in our lives and in our homes by being the Master of all of our living!

TODAY'S BIBLE READING: Isaiah 53:1-13

51.
A CHILD IS ON LOAN

"I'll lend you for a little time
a child of mine," He said,
"For you to love the while he lives
and mourn for when he's dead.
It may be six or seven years
or twenty-two or three,
But will you, till I call him back,
take care of him for me?
He'll bring his charms to gladden you,
And should his stay be brief,
You'll have his lovely memories
As solace for your grief.

"I cannot promise he will stay,
Since all from earth return,
But there are lessons taught down there
I want this child to learn.
I've looked this wide world over
In My search for teachers true,
And from the throngs that crowd life's lanes
I have selected you;
Now will you give him all your love
Not think the labor vain,
Nor hate Me when I come to call
and take him back again?"

I fancied that I heard them say, "Dear Lord, Thy will be done,
For all the joy the child shall bring, the risk of grief we'll run.
We'll shelter him with tenderness, we'll love him while we may,
And for the happiness we've known, forever grateful stay.
But should the angels call for him much sooner than we planned
We'll brave the bitter grief that comes and try to understand."

(Author is unknown)

The following short paragraph was written by Vance Havner: "God uses broken things. It takes broken soil to produce a crop, broken clouds to give rain, broken grain to give bread, broken bread to give strength. It is the broken alabaster box that gives forth perfume . . . it is Peter, weeping bitterly, who returns to greater power than ever."

Why? I don't have an answer. It's one of those mysteries known only to God. But in our pain and brokenness there is a source of new life. Out of this process of the human soul comes a life of maturity. If anything is learned in this life . . . it's that the things that seem to break us are in reality the things that make us. There was a cross even in the heart of God.

There is one Bible verse which has caused me more question than any other that comes to mind. Find it in Hebrews 5:8, "Although He was a Son, He learned obedience from what He suffered." How is that possible that even the perfect, sinless Son of God walked through the school of pain? Whatever the mystery and whatever the reason . . . from this, we have just read that He learned obedience in and through the crucible of pain.

And in the best and worst sense of the meaning . . . each child is only on loan. If you do your job as a mother, that child will one day leave the nest to fly on his own. If the child is taken from you, prematurely, that child, too, is on loan. Therefore, while we have the privilege, while we have the loaned child, our responsibility, our God-given responsibility is to prepare that child for life and death. To give that child our legacy of love with a grateful heart, fulfilling, with God's help, that wonderful privilege of being a parent.

TODAY'S BIBLE READING: I Kings 17:1-24

52.
LEFTOVERS

Thank you for sticking with it and working your way through all the previous 51 chapters. My hope is that you have made some new discoveries about life and living. Perhaps your horizons have been enriched in some small way.

Then . . . as any good cook knows, no matter how carefully you concoct your meal planning, inevitably there are leftovers, bits and pieces of this and that, barrel scrappings . . . all of which lead us to this final chapter. These are some of the things too good to simply throw out. Perhaps you can warm these up like a leftover hot dish and serve them again. Enjoy this potpourri.

The bathtub was invented in 1850. The telephone was invented in 1875. That means if you'd been living in 1850 you could have sat in the bathtub for 25 years without the phone ringing!

IN AN EMERGENCY

It seems that a mother mouse felt that the time had come to introduce her baby mice to the larger world. So, having cautioned them that they must pay very strict attention to what their mother does, she proceeded to lead them out of their comfortable mouse hole. Upon leaving the hole and entering the living room she suddenly saw the big house cat sleeping a few yards away in the middle of her intended path. Frightened at what lay ahead, but not wanting to appear cowardly to her children, the mouse led her family silently forward.

Just as she was creeping past the sleeping cat, the cat's eyes popped open and she raised her paw to strike. What was Mother Mouse to do to save her children from danger? As the paw began its downward swipe, Mother Mouse turned on the cat and barked like a dog. The cat was so frightened she turned and ran. Whereupon the Mother Mouse turned to her baby mice and said, "In an emergency, it's always good to know a second language!"

COMMUNICATION . . . ALL FOULED UP

A mature-looking lady made an appointment with a marriage counselor and told her flat out, "I would like to divorce my husband."

To this, the counselor replied, "Well, do you have any grounds?"

She answered, "Why yes. We have almost an acre."

The puzzled counselor tried again, "You didn't understand. What I want to know is do you and your husband have a grudge?"

The lady answered, "Actually, we don't, but we do have a nice carport."

At this the counselor shook her head and replied, "Ma'am, I'm sorry, but I just don't see any reason why you should divorce your husband."

The lady looked at the counselor and said, "It's just that he can't carry on an intelligent conversation."

A NOVEL NEW PROGRAM FOR KIDS

The local Parent-Teacher Association group was involved in a serious discussion about what the school's students could do after school was dismissed for the day. Among the many suggestions made were: playgrounds, youth huts, bicycle trails, video viewing, youth canteen, and a student center with paid supervision. Finally, a practical gray-haired grandmother who had heard enough, quietly asked, "Couldn't they just go home?"

ON AGING

Great-Aunt Lucy had become somewhat hard of hearing and while at her annual checkup her doctor recommended she see a specialist. The specialist suggested that she submit to an operation to improve her hearing. But she promptly vetoed the idea by saying: "I'm 94 years old, and I've heard enough."

WHAT DID YOU SAY?

It seems this woman called 911 in great agitation. She shouted, "Come as quickly as you can, my house is on fire!"

"Okay, lady, okay," said the dispatcher, calmly, "just tell us how to get there."

"Oh . . ." she paused for a moment, "Don't you have your little yellow trucks, anymore?"

GOING THE SECOND MILE

A traveling salesman called his wife from a coin-operated phone in a distant city, finished the conversation, said goodbye and replaced the receiver. As he was walking away, the phone rang. He went back and answered it, expecting to be informed of extra charges. But the operator said, "I thought you'd like to know. Just after you hung up, your wife said, 'I love you.' "*(On the Upbeat)*

THE REAL CHOICE

You don't get to choose how you're going to die. Or when. You only decide how you're going to live. Now! (Joan Baez)

THE LAST WORD . . . DON'T QUIT!

A mother, wishing to encourage her young son's progress at the piano, bought tickets for a Paderewski performance. When the night arrived, they found their seats near the front of the concert hall and eyed the majestic, black Steinway waiting on stage. Soon the mother found a friend to talk with and the son slipped away. When eight o'clock arrived, the spotlights came on, the audience quieted, and only then did they notice the boy up on the bench, innocently picking out, "Twinkle, Twinkle, Little Star." His mother gasped, but before she could retrieve her son, the master appeared on the stage and quickly moved to the keyboard.

He whispered to the little boy, "Don't quit . . . keep playing." Leaning over, Paderewski reached down with his left hand and began filling in a bass part. Soon his right arm reached around the other side, encircling the child, to add a running obbligato. Together, the old master and the young novice held the crowd mesmerized![26]

In our lives, unpolished as we may be, it is the Master who surrounds us and whispers in our ear, time and time again: "DON'T QUIT . . . KEEP PLAYING!" And as we do, He augments, supplements, supplies, nurtures, and gives until a life of amazing beauty is created! The life of a mother!

TODAY'S BIBLE READING: Revelation 22:1-21

ENDNOTES

[1] Erma Bombeck, *Parables, Etc.*, Saratoga Press, May 1984, p. 1, adapted.

[2] Paul Brand and Philip Yancey, *Fearfully and Wonderfully Made* (Grand Rapids, MI: Zondervan, 1980).

[3] Larry Christensen, "The Christian Family," as it appeared in *Parables, Etc.,* May 1985, adapted.

[4] Leo Tolstoy.

[5] Wayne Rouse, *The Pastor's Story File*, April 1996.

[6] Ken Dolan, *Straight Talk on Your Money*, vol. 5, no. 5, p. 1, adapted.

[7] *Illustration Digest*, Number 1, 1966, p. 2, adapted.

[8] Dr. Paul Brand and Philip Yancey, *In His Image* (Grand Rapids, MI: Judith Markham Books, Zondervan Publishing House, 1987), p. 43–46.

[9] William Goodin, *God Laughs, Too* (Lima, OH: C.S.S. Pub. Co., 1990).

[10] All of the poetry in Chapter 19 is by Robert R. Hostetler.

[11] John Jackson, *Monday Morning*, (Indianapolis, IN, October 10, 1988).

[12] *Success* magazine, 8/86, adapted, p.36-37.

[13] Jon H. Allen, editor, *Illustration Digest*, #4, 1995.

[14] Bob Vallier, *The Pastor's Story File*, May 1986.

[15] William Jones, *The Pastor's Story File*, November 1977.

[16] *Motherhood: the Second Oldest Profession.*

[17] Anthony Campolo, *The Power Delusion* (Wheaton, IL: Victor Books, 1983), p. 30-31.

[18] All poetry in Chapter 42 is from *The Speaker's Treasury of 400 Quotable Poems* (Grand Rapids, MI: Zondervan, 1965).

[19] Maxwell Anderson, *Anne of a Thousand Days.*

[20] Nick Stinnett and John DeFrain, *Secrets of Strong Families.*

[21] Karen Cavaleri, *The Pastor's Story File*, March 1985.

[22] Nancy L. Dahlberg, *The Pastor's Story File*, December 1985.

[23] Jon H. Allen, editor, *Illustration Digest*, No. 2, 1996.

[24] Peter Stoner, *Science Speaks*.

[25] Unknown, James S. Hewett, editor, *Illustrations Unlimited* (Wheaton, IL: Tyndale House, 1988).

[26] James. S. Hewett, editor, *Parables, Etc.*, Saratoga Press, Nov. 1983.